Minding the Money

Minding the Money

A Practical Guide for Volunteer Treasurers

of…

religious organizations
charitable funds
neighborhood associations
men's and women's
garden clubs
professional societies
political committees
fraternities and sororities
student clubs
sports clubs
fraternal lodges
local unions
hobby clubs
social clubs
investment clubs
etc.

Alden Todd and Joseph M. Galloway

ASJA Press
New York Lincoln Shanghai

Minding the Money
A Practical Guide for Volunteer Treasurers

ASJA Press
an imprint of iUniverse, Inc.

For information address:
iUniverse
2021 Pine Lake Road, Suite 100
Lincoln, NE 68512
www.iuniverse.com

ISBN: 0-595-27262-2

Printed in the United States of America

Contents

No Stereotyping Intended ix
Introduction xi

PART I 1
Chapter 1.   What is the Treasurer's Job? 3
Chapter 2.   Selecting the Treasurer 8
Chapter 3.   The Treasurer as Officer and Board Member 17
Chapter 4.   Financial Record-Keeping 26
Chapter 5.   The Treasurer as Business Manager 44
Chapter 6.   Business Dealings with Outsiders .71
Chapter 7.   Relations with the Membership 85
Chapter 8.   Dealing with Employees 93

PART II 105
A.   Forming a New Organization 107
B.   Obtaining and Retaining Tax-exempt Status 114
C.   Payroll Taxes 125
D.   Checklist of Reports and Payments 131
E.   Single or Double Entry Bookkeeping? 135
F.   Cash or Accrual Method? 138
G.   Blocking Frauds and Theft 144
H.   Finding Errors 149
I.   Preparing the Annual Financial Report .152
J.   Handling the IRS Audit 161
K.   Change of Association's Name 170
L.   Changing the Association Financial System 172
M.   Using Computers 175
N.   Using Bank Payroll Services 179
O.   Unrelated Business Income Tax 181
P.   Fund Accounting 189
Q.   Private Foundations 195
R.   Charitable Contributions 199
The Authors 209
Index 211

To all those volunteers who faithfully mind the money

No Stereotyping Intended

In this book the authors have adopted the convention of referring to the association treasurer as "he" only to avoid tripping over more pronouns than necessary. They recognize, of course, that many association treasurers are women. No stereotyping is intended.

INTRODUCTION

Why This Book?

For more than a century since the publication of *Robert's Rules of Order* in 1876, there have been accepted rules of parliamentary procedure that are followed by presiding officers of associations and meetings throughout the English-speaking world. However, there has been no corresponding guide governing the functions of an association treasurer. Nor has there been a generally-accepted book of instruction from which a new treasurer can learn his various duties and how to perform them.

Some national organizations have issued their own programs of financial record-keeping and reporting which local or chapter treasurers are expected to follow. But in most instances such programs have been designed to meet the particular needs of one organization, and are not suitable for general application to a wide variety of associations.

Minding the Money is intended for not-for-profit organizations of all kinds that do not have an established system of financial management or clearly written procedures for their treasurer to follow. This is probably the case with a majority of the voluntary associations in our society. Some may have provisions in their constitution and bylaws specifying certain duties of the treasurer, but these provisions usually cover only a small part of the treasurer's job. Most of it is left unexplained. Too often, after a treasurer is elected or appointed to office, he is given brief instruction by his predecessor on the way things were done up to that point, and then is left to shift for himself.

This book outlines for treasurers the range of responsibilities they should be prepared to assume, sometimes on their own initiative, if these have not been spelled out beforehand. It points out to association governing boards how they should go about selecting a treasurer, determining his duties and authority, and exercising effective control over his performance. And it reminds association officers and the membership what they have a right to expect from their elected or appointed treasurer. *Minding the Money*, therefore, is a book for everyone who takes an active interest in directing a voluntary association; it is not for the treasurer alone.

Part I of this book, consisting of Chapters 1–8, is designed for new treasurers of smaller organizations and for those that have not yet had the years of experience that have led to established, smoothly-operating methods of running the treasury. Part II of this book is devoted to issues that concern the larger organizations whose operations have become more complex than they once were. Many of these associations may have professional management. Some of the matters discussed in Part I lead logically to a related discussion at a more complex level in Part II. Readers who find some of Part II useful to their organization can discover the relevant sections easily enough. They were separated from the basic material in Part I because many of them do not apply to the inexperienced treasurer or to the new or small organization for which this book is largely intended.

The purpose of *Minding the Money*, like that of *Robert's Rules of Order*, is to fill a felt need of our time—that of thousands of men and women who each year become treasurer of an association, club, student organization or other group, and who need help. The parallel to *Robert's Rules of Order* should not be drawn too closely, however. The author of that work, General Henry M. Robert, codified the rules of conducting meetings which became accepted by all kinds of organizations as binding on them. *Minding the Money*, in contrast, is not intended to impose rules that must be followed. Rather, it offers practical guidance to both general principles and specific situations in handling the finances of associations. It is left to each treasurer and organization to decide what in these pages serves it best.

PART I

Chapter 1. WHAT IS THE TREASURER'S JOB?

(A)   Financial Record-Keeping

(B)   Business Management

(C)   Business Dealings with Outsiders

(D)   Relations with the Membership

(E)   Dealing with Employees

CHAPTER 1

What is the Treasurer's Job?

Put most simply, the treasurer is the financial officer of the association, responsible for the receipt, care and disbursement of its funds. From this bare statement of duties there extend a number of specific responsibilities that are commonly regarded as belonging to the treasurer: financial record-keeping, business management, dealing with outsiders, handling membership relations, and dealing with employees. Some organizations may assign one or more of these functions to another officer, a committee or an individual. They are outlined here as the treasurer's duties because, more often than not, they fall to him. Later chapters discuss in detail each of these five aspects of the association treasurer's job.

(A)   Financial Record-Keeping

The treasurer is responsible for keeping accurate records of funds received by the association, of money spent from its treasury, and of the financial assets of the association that are invested or in safekeeping. The records should be kept in such detail as the governing board wishes, and as the needs of the organization dictate.

If the association has an office, its financial records should be kept there. If it has no office, the treasurer should see to the safe maintenance of the financial records at his own residence or place of work, or elsewhere according to the circumstances.

The treasurer should see that the financial records are kept as current as practical. If the association has an office staff, the treasurer is responsible for supervising the staff in keeping all the records current, or for keeping them current himself.

At intervals specified by the association, the treasurer should be prepared to report on the financial state of the organization.

An outgoing treasurer should turn over to his successor all financial records of the association, current and in good order. He should offer whatever explanation of the records is necessary to ensure that the transition is smooth and complete.

(B)   Business Management

As a logical and expected extension of financial record-keeping, the treasurer assumes the role of business manager of an association, responsible for decisions and actions to keep it financially sound. In some organizations he may be the only officer who takes on this responsibility. In others he may act as adviser to the president or the governing board, who then decide on actions to be taken. As business manager, the treasurer should read the temper of the group accurately so that he does his full duty in steering its financial course without exceeding his proper authority and acting as a financial dictator. The extent of the treasurer's authority is set by the bylaws and the customs of each organization, and not by the treasurer's title.

Although it is not always possible in a new and growing association, the treasurer should try to establish a budget—a planned program of expenditures with the means of financing them. The budget grows from the program of the association, and therefore should be designed to further that program within the limits of funds available. When there is no planned program, the treasurer should try to influence the governing board to establish a budget for a fixed period ahead (usually a year), and then see that the budget adopted is realistic.

As business manager, the treasurer should take responsibility for setting up internal controls over the handling of association finances. In this role, he should aim for accuracy and efficiency as well as defending against theft. The treasurer should enlist the full cooperation of members and staff employees in following the control procedures he sets up, especially when dealing with people who are less alert than he is as to what can go wrong. He sometimes must explain that his object in setting internal controls over the handling of funds is to protect the organization, not himself, and that most standard controls have proven their effectiveness through the years. If necessary, he should call on the governing board to give him firm backing in putting desirable controls into effect.

The treasurer is often the first to observe financial trends in operation. One of his most important duties is to monitor such trends and report them at the proper time to the governing board or other officers concerned. This enables the association to take action, if needed, before a small loss grows into a serious one. It is not enough for the treasurer to keep careful records of increasing losses, of which the governing board is not aware, and then report sadly at the end of the year that the organization had a losing year financially. He should be alert to changes and report them promptly.

(C)   Business Dealings with Outsiders

The treasurer represents the association in business dealings with companies, agencies and individuals outside its ranks. The number of such outsiders with whom he deals varies widely from one organization to another, and depends on the complexity of its operations. The following are among the most common:

Vendors:	The treasurer checks incoming vendors' bills for goods and services, and sees that they are paid.
Banks, Savings Institutions:	The treasurer signs all association checks, supervises bank deposits, reconciles monthly bank statements and monitors investment accounts.
Landlord, Tenants:	The treasurer sees that the office rent is paid on time, and reviews the lease at renewal. If the association sublets out part of its space, he is responsible for financial relations with the tenant.
Tax Agencies:	If the association has employees, the treasurer is responsible for timely payment of withheld wage taxes (federal and state) and FICA (Social Security) taxes. He files the required reports on taxes paid. He is also responsible for paying any other taxes owed by the association.
Insurance Carriers:	The treasurer should see that the association has adequate insurance of the right kinds, and keeps coverage up-to-date.
Accountants:	Where necessary, the treasurer should obtain professional accounting services for the association, and should also seek the accountant's constructive suggestions for improving the association's financial system.

In addition, the treasurer may deal with attorneys, computer service bureaus, a state registration agency, the Internal Revenue Service, donors who contribute to the association, and others.

(D)   Relations with the Membership

Relations between the treasurer and individual members of an association center most frequently around payment of dues. The treasurer may in some cases be required to pursue some members in order to collect back dues, and also payment for services or special events for which credit was extended. And he may need to ask a member for a second payment because the member's check was dishonored by the bank for lack of sufficient funds.

Outside the routine collections, to which members are accustomed, the treasurer's role as collector for the association can sometimes turn into an embarrassing and unhappy one. For this reason, a treasurer should be backed up by clearly announced collection procedures established by the governing board. This may help him avoid personal antagonism from disgruntled delinquents.

The treasurer is called upon at intervals to speak for the governing board in explaining the association's financial position to members. In answering members' questions, he should be as candid as the rules and customs of the organization permit so that members will have no reason to think that anything is being hidden from them. In this way he promotes their confidence in him and his fellow officers.

(E)   Dealing with Employees

Whereas other people in an association may direct staff employees in their non-financial duties, the treasurer should supervise that part of their work relating to finances. This involves the association's bookkeeping, bank deposits, and any other work assigned to the staff in support of the treasurer's function.

Unless the responsibility is assigned elsewhere, the treasurer should see that staff members are paid on time, and that a careful record is kept of payroll deductions for taxes and other purposes. The treasurer should take part in setting association policy on both salaries and non-salary benefits for the paid staff because these items constitute a major association expense.

Chapter 2. SELECTING THE TREASURER

(A)   Positive Attributes
    (1)   Integrity, Honesty
    (2)   Interest and Responsibility
    (3)   Money Sense
    (4)   Available Time
    (5)   Clear Handwriting

(B)   Negative Attributes
    (1)   The Lone Operator
    (2)   The Type Who Fails to Report
    (3)   The Too-Eager Candidate
    (4)   The Financially Incompetent Type

(C)   Two Traps to Avoid
    (1)   The "Best Friend" Syndrome
    (2)   The Dog in the Manger

(D)   Training Period as Assistant Treasurer

CHAPTER 2

Selecting the Treasurer

Selecting a member to serve an association as treasurer should be done with care. The position should not be given to just anyone who is available and willing. More than any other officer, the treasurer often carries out much of his work without conferring with other officers or members. He may be in a position, if he is not the right person for the job, to do the association considerable damage before anyone else knows about it. It is therefore important for an organization to seek out the right individual for treasurer, even if he must be persuaded or drafted to accept the treasurership, rather than choose the readily available candidate about whom there are doubts.

There is, of course, always a human element involved in selecting anyone for any responsibility. A nominating committee or a governing board can never be certain that a given member would become an excellent treasurer, even though he seems to meet all the requirements. But it is certainly wise to measure the qualifications of a candidate for treasurer against both the positive and negative attributes of association treasurers that have been proven through the years. Very few people can fit the qualifications perfectly, and therefore certain shortcomings may have to be accepted. But at least they should be considered in the selection process.

(A)   Positive Attributes

(1)   Integrity, Honesty

This is the premier consideration in selecting the treasurer. The difficulty comes from our being inclined to take one another at face value and to presume that our colleagues are honest, unless we have direct evidence to the contrary. Yet in most associations it is difficult to say with certainty that a fellow member is thoroughly honest, especially when the members do not know each other very well and do not deal with one another in situations where honesty can be tested.

In addition, most people hesitate to say, or even hint, that they are not sure of the honesty of a fellow member, even in the intimacy of a meeting of officers or of the nominating committee. We do not want to be unfair or to injure another person's reputation. Nor do we want to become known as a spreader of rumors. So it frequently happens that we can be uneasy about a given person becoming the treasurer because of certain limited observations of his attitudes and behavior, yet we suppress our feelings. We may say to ourselves that just because the member under consideration may have cut corners with his taxes or in his business dealings, this is no reason to think he will be careless with an association's funds. So we often remain silent.

Exactly how one should explain his doubts to others in the nominating group is a matter of diplomacy to be worked out in each situation. Perhaps one can carefully express such feelings in confidence to one other member to see whether that other person also has doubts that he, too, is suppressing. If that turns out to be the case, two people are in a better position than one to suggest that another name be considered. In any event, it does an association no good for a member or officer to suppress his doubts about a candidate's honesty, only to regret later that he failed to express them.

(2)   Interest and Responsibility

The treasurer should be someone who is genuinely interested in the association and feels a sense of responsibility to it, if he is to devote the necessary time and effort to carrying out the treasurer's duties well. He must be conscientious. He must care. This is not a job for the self-promoter who is eager to become prominent in the organization and sees the treasurership as a convenient stepping-stone to the presidency. If his primary goal is self-aggrandizement, he may be unwilling to carry out the detailed work that does not bring applause.

Nor is it a job for the careless operator. The treasurer should be willing to take pains with record-keeping, to follow up on details, to be alert to situations that call for investigation. He should have the temperament that insists on nailing things down.

(3)   Money Sense

The treasurer should have a systematic, thorough way of handling business affairs and money. This does not necessarily mean he must be someone from the business or financial world. Of course, it helps a great deal to have as treasurer a member with business or financial experience because he will already have learned some of the basic procedures that a good treasurer should master. But the other qualities should be present also.

The treasurer with money sense has a sense of proportion. He understands the importance of keeping a close watch on income and expenditures, and he sees accurately how they fit into the association's operating program. He does things on time. He keeps clear records. He confers regularly with fellow officers. He can see which purchases are reasonable and which ones do not make sense. And he knows when to ring the alarm bell.

Therefore, an association may consider first as candidates for treasurer those members who have experience in running a business, keeping business records, dealing with banks, handling tax matters, and the like. But the experience such people have gained from their working lives should not be the sole criterion by which a treasurer is chosen.

Better to elect an honest, conscientious member with an inborn money sense but without business experience than to choose someone from the business world who lacks the other important qualities.

(4) Available Time

The candidate for treasurer must be able to give adequate time to the office. There is no advantage in giving the treasurership to someone who must squeeze in the treasurer's duties between other commitments that are more important to him. In a pinch between the requirements of his livelihood, those of his family, and those of his voluntary association, the volunteer treasurership is likely to be neglected, even though the treasurer had the best of intentions at the beginning and is well qualified otherwise.

A certified public accountant, for example, might be the best trained person in an association to become its treasurer. But if the heaviest load of the treasurer's year-end work should fall during the CPA's so-called "busy season" (January 1–April 15), the CPA might not be able to give the proper attention to his voluntary treasurership. The same might be true of a salesman or an executive who must make frequent out-of-town trips. If a member who must often be away from the association's headquarters city is proposed for treasurer, there should be a frank inquiry into how much his absence would interfere with his treasurer's duties.

(5) Clear Handwriting

Every entry in the association books should be written so that it is clearly legible. This is particularly true in a small organization in which the treasurer keeps the financial records in his own handwriting. If any abbreviations or symbols are used in the records, an explanation of them should be written in an appropriate place. The records are the property of the association, not of the treasurer, and therefore should be kept in such a manner that they can be read by anyone, without mistake or confusion. A treasurer who does not observe this simple rule is not doing his duty by the organization and is being unfair to the succeeding treasurer.

If a person who is otherwise well qualified to be treasurer is physically or temperamentally unable to write in a clear hand, he should direct a clerical assistant in making record entries and take full responsibility for their accuracy.

(B) Negative Attributes

Just as there are positive characteristics that an association nominating group should look for in a prospective treasurer, there are also certain well-known negative attributes that mark the unsuitable candidate. Prominent among them are the following:

(1) The Lone Operator

This is the kind of person who resents being questioned, who views almost any questioning as a reflection on either his honesty or his efficiency. He sees anyone's inquiry about the treasury as an inquisition, or even an attack on him. He tries to let no one else in on the mystery over which he presides, treating his position as if it were a priestly function beyond the understanding of ordinary members. He resents, and often resists, any review of his work by other officers or by a committee. In short, he is not cooperative in his relations with his fellow officers, the office staff or the membership.

A treasurer might, by chance, be the lone operator type and still be efficient and honest. But if he lets no one know what he is doing and how he is carrying out his responsibilities, the association may not know until too late whether or not he is handling his office well. He may. But, on the other hand, he may be doing a very poor job of record-keeping, making tax payments, and carrying out other duties, and his lone-operator temperament keeps his shortcomings hidden from others. In selecting a treasurer, therefore, those in charge of nominations should make certain that the candidate they put forward is willing to work cooperatively with others and understands that the treasurership is not a private affair.

(2) The Type Who Fails to Report

Even if the treasurer is willing to discuss financial matters freely and is glad to answer questions, he still owes his colleagues financial reports at regular intervals. Some treasurers, however, never seem to have a prepared report for a scheduled meeting of the executive body or of the membership. Such treasurers may be temperamentally unwilling to take the trouble to prepare a written report. Others do not see why they should bother. And in some cases the executive body may not inform the new treasurer that he is expected to present a financial report at stated intervals. An inexperienced president, or one hard-pressed by many items of business, may get in the habit of omitting a financial report from the agenda of meetings. Under such conditions, the treasurer who is not inclined to prepare a report feels no compulsion to do so, and consequently may neglect this duty for a long period.

When selecting a candidate for treasurer, a nominating group should make it clear that responsible, regular reporting on the financial condition of the association is an important part of the job. The content of such reports, their degree of detail and their frequency will vary from one association to another according to its needs. The important point is that the prospective treasurer understands this responsibility. If he does not, or gives evidence of being a non-reporting type, he can be a poor choice.

(3)   The Too-Eager Candidate

When an association treasurer is being selected, the common pattern is for the nominating group to search for likely candidates—and sometimes to have great difficulty finding even one who seems right for the post and who is willing to accept it. However, there are times when a member presents himself as willing and eager to help the organization. Either subtly or directly he may push his own name forward as a prospective treasurer. Because the office is difficult to fill, the nominating body may view such an offer as manna from heaven. They may welcome the volunteer warmly and virtually thrust the treasurership into his hands without further thought.

However, it is sound policy to think carefully about any such offer to serve. Of course, many an honest member may volunteer to take on one of the time-consuming tasks of running an association, and the treasurership is certainly that. At the same time, the person whose motives are not so honest may think that once he is within easy reach of the treasury, he can take advantage of it with no one the wiser. So the treasurership is a natural objective for one who has theft in mind. For this reason, it is better for the office to seek the man. An over-eager person should not be given the office by default. This is not to condemn everyone who volunteers to undertake the demanding job of treasurer. It is, rather, a common-sense warning based on what has been observed in the past.

A corollary would be to warn against permitting a treasurer to serve too many terms successively. One should be especially wary of the treasurer who wants to stay in the position year after year. Rotation of treasurers after a stated period should be the rule in every association. This follows a policy in many businesses where certain positions are vulnerable to collusion with outsiders.

(4)   The Financially Incompetent Type

A person who has been unable to manage his own financial affairs competently is certainly a very poor prospect for managing the affairs of an association. The member who has been through bankruptcies or has been unable to meet alimony or child support payments does not suddenly become fully responsible when it comes to taking charge of the membership's money. So if financial incompetence or irresponsibility is in the record of a member being considered for treasurer, the nominating group should pass on to other names.

The same would hold true for the compulsive gambler, who might otherwise seem like a promising candidate. Unless he is wealthy, the inveterate gambler can be flush one week and broke the next—with the broke periods being the more frequent. Under these circumstances, it is extremely unwise for such a person to be within easy reach of the association's money, which he might think of "borrowing" only long enough to recoup his losses.

(C)   Two Traps to Avoid

After a nominating committee has considered a possible treasurer in light of the desirable and undesirable qualities discussed above, even the candidate with a near-perfect score on these points may turn out to be a bad choice. The following are two potentially dangerous situations that bear watching.

(1)   The "Best Friend" Syndrome

Often a member will say that a candidate for treasurer is his "best friend" whom he has known for years and would trust with all his possessions. This reasoning leads to the result that the treasurer's work is not closely supervised and his qualifications, or lack thereof, are glossed over. Of course, this overlooks the possibility that the person may be a slick embezzler who has hoodwinked his acquaintances over the years. Almost invariably such white-collar criminals have a number of unsuspecting, law-abiding citizens as their good friends. Unfortunately, such individuals are more numerous than we think, and when they are exposed, their dishonesty comes as a shock to most of their friends. Fortunately, however, these criminals would rather try to steal the funds of a large business instead of a small club treasury. Nevertheless, they will often take small amounts, too, if it looks easy.

A more common threat to organizations comes from the person who never had any criminal intentions at all, at least not to begin with. This person is an average, clean-living citizen who would never dream of committing an outright theft. Yet he can get in a financial bind, need some cash for what he thinks will be "just a little while" and see the club dollars sitting idly in a checking account. Of course, he would rather not "borrow" the association's funds for his own purposes, but he fears that his utilities will be shut off, or his car repossessed, or his stocks sold to meet a margin call, or his business ruined if he doesn't get some cash—fast. He sees the association's funds just sitting there, doing no one any good, and he finally decides to borrow them with the intention of repaying as soon as the crisis has passed. No harm done, he thinks, and nobody will know the difference.

The light-fingered treasurer is not some unrealistic, hypothetical goblin conjured up by your authors. One of your authors had a good friend to whom he would have confidently given the key to his house and with whom he had worked as a partner on several projects. This friend became the treasurer of a county political committee and soon found that one of his other business interests was unable to meet a payroll. He borrowed from the party treasury, met the payroll, and then repaid the funds before anyone found out. No harm done! Shortly afterwards, though, someone did discover the loan and the individual had to resign amid a series of humiliating newspaper stories. He barely escaped prosecution.

This particular story ends here because the loan was discovered early. But in many cases there is no early discovery. Even if the treasurer repays the money, he often finds that he needs more money again. Since nothing bad happened the first time, the pressure to repay is less. He borrows more and more money. He still has a fantasy about repaying everything, but the situation gets out of control. He desperately covers up to forestall the day of reckoning. Eventually the shortage is discovered, but by then all the borrowed money is gone and the club is the victim. Thus, someone's "best friend," who never meant to steal anything, has ruined the club and possibly his own career because the association failed to take a few common-sense steps that could have prevented this tragedy from ever starting.

(2)   The Dog in the Manger

Another threat to an organization comes from a treasurer who is completely honest, who would not take or even borrow a penny for personal purposes. Yet this treasurer, through ignorance, incompetence, laziness or some other shortcoming, does a poor job as treasurer and yet insists on keeping the position year after year as if it were a personal possession. He doesn't carry out his duties properly, but he won't let anyone else perform them either—thus the name, dog in the manger.

Poor work can manifest itself in many ways. Erroneous financial statements, costly tax violations, bad investments, wasteful purchases, annoyed members—these can all harm an organization just as much as an embezzlement. And if the bumbling treasurer has assistants, they may be stealing from the organization even if the treasurer is personally honest.

How can such a misfitted person ever get, and keep, his position as treasurer? It happens easily and often. Because the election of officers is frequently a popularity contest, a well-liked, unqualified person can get the job through the "Best Friend" Syndrome. He is there, he is willing to serve, so he accepts. Once he is in office, reelection may become a routine formality, especially if the person openly asks to keep the job. Then the other members are put in the position of either voting their approval or losing a friend—or many friends if the treasurer has loyal allies. In this situation most people would choose the path of least resistance and vote to reelect the treasurer, at least if there were no proof of fraud or imminent bankruptcy of the club.

(D)   Training Period as Assistant Treasurer

Some associations require so much work from the treasurer that it makes sense to call on another member to act as his deputy, or assistant treasurer. Where this is done, the deputy can be chosen not only to help the incumbent treasurer, but also to serve an informal apprenticeship for the treasurer's job in the next administration. The abilities and work methods of the assistant treasurer can be observed over a period of months. If they are of the right sort, this member's period of service as assistant treasurer can remove much of the guesswork from the process of selecting the next treasurer. If, on the other hand, the member does not handle the job of deputy well, the association can learn about his weaknesses in time to avoid nominating him as treasurer for the term to follow.

Chapter 3. THE TREASURER AS OFFICER AND BOARD MEMBER

(A) Liaison Between Outgoing and Incoming Treasurer
    (1) Listing Bank Accounts, Investment Funds
    (2) Changing Authorized Signatures for Banks
    (3) Arranging for Facsimile Signatures

(B) Regular Financial Reports
    (1) Clarity of Financial Reports
    (2) Paying Attention to Treasurer's Reports
    (3) When the Treasurer Fails to Report

(C) The Treasurer as Financial Educator
    (1) Accuracy in Reporting Figures
    (2) Interpreting the Bank Balance

(D) Compensating and Reimbursing the Treasurer

CHAPTER 3

The Treasurer as Officer and Board Member

(A)   Liaison Between Outgoing and Incoming Treasurer

The responsibility for successful liaison between the outgoing and the incoming treasurer rests on both. In order for treasury functions to continue smoothly upon a change of officers, it is important for the outgoing treasurer to meet with his successor to explain how the duties of the office have been carried out so far. If the association's financial management is complex, the liaison process may require several meetings, and perhaps some follow-up telephone calls.

Explanations should cover these points, where applicable: The treasury filing system; methods of keeping records of cash receipts and disbursements; procedures for paying bills; the checking account; investment funds; procedures for paying staff salaries; withheld payroll taxes and system of payment; quarterly and year-end reports due to the Internal Revenue Service and the state tax agency; financial reporting to the governing board and the membership; the association insurance program—and anything else relevant to the job.

It is irresponsible for either the old or the new treasurer to neglect this process of instruction. The outgoing treasurer owes it to the organization and to his successor to arrange all records neatly and mark them plainly before passing them on. He should be patient in his explanations and generous with his time in helping the new treasurer understand the present procedures. On his side, the incoming treasurer should take notes on everything that is not plainly documented so he will not neglect a duty he was told about but which he might forget.

(1)   Listing Bank Accounts, Investment Funds

The new treasurer should obtain from the outgoing treasurer a complete list of all of the association's bank accounts, money-market funds, bonds, certificates of deposit, petty cash and other property of value. The list should include the names of all financial institutions concerned, with the relevant account numbers, addresses, names of contact persons and telephone numbers. The incoming treasurer should also receive all bank books, checkbooks, files and anything else necessary for a responsible transfer of custody from one treasurer to another.

The outgoing treasurer, when preparing to leave office, should draw up such a list for his successor and deliver it with the related files along with whatever explanation is required.

Report of Association Bank Accounts and Investment Funds

CHECKING ACCOUNT:

_____   _____   _____
(Name of bank)   (Address)   (Telephone)

Bank Account No.: _____

See file folder "Banks - (name of bank)"

INVESTMENT FUND:

_____   _____   _____
(Name of fund)   (Address)   (Telephone)

Account No.: _____

See file folder "Investment Fund - (name of fund)"

There are no other banks or investment funds with association assets.

                                                        _____
                                                        (Signature)

                                Treasurer   _____
                                                                (Date)

---

(2)   Changing Authorized Signatures for Banks

Before a change of association officers, the outgoing treasurer should take the initiative to notify the organization's bank of the coming change. Usually a bank requires the signing of new authorization cards by the treasurer, the president and anyone else who will sign checks for the association, so that the bank has the proper signatures on file. It may also require a signed resolution adopted by the governing board to validate the new authorization cards. When delivering the cards and resolution to the bank, the treasurer should include a letter specifying the date on which the new signatures become valid on association checks. The treasurer should follow a similar procedure with all other financial institutions with which the association does business, such as the custodians of its investment funds. This can easily be overlooked because the treasurer has not had such frequent dealings with these institutions as he has with the checking account bank.

After the change of authorized signatures has been made, the treasurer should report this fact to the next meeting of the governing board so that the transfer can be recorded in the minutes.

(3) Arranging for Facsimile Signatures

On occasion, convenience requires that the signature of an incoming association officer be applied to checks in facsimile with a rubber stamp rather than being signed with pen and ink. In such a case, the outgoing treasurer, in cooperation with his successor, should see that the governing board adopts a resolution authorizing the use of the facsimile signature. Then the resolution and a sample of the facsimile signature should be furnished to the bank, because many banks require this procedure as a protection both to the bank and to the depositor, which is the association.

The treasurer should see to it that the signature stamp is kept secure under responsible custody, and that no one but the authorized person uses it. Where both the treasurer's signature and the facsimile signature of another officer are required (*e.g.*, on a check), the treasurer should not apply the stamped signature himself. This should be done by a second person, such as the head of the office staff, so that person can see the check before it is sent to the payee. The treasurer should also see that the governing board designates a custodian of the signature stamp, and authorizes a deputy to apply it when the custodian is not available.

(B) Regular Financial Reports

The members of an association always have the right to know what is happening to their money. The treasurer should therefore be required to report at established intervals to the governing board and to the membership on the association's financial status. Such a requirement is best included in the association's bylaws, where it can become known to all members and officers. A treasurer or a governing board that resists informing the membership on the state of the association's finances undermines the members' confidence in the honesty or competence of their elected officers.

The intervals at which such reports should be made, and the form in which they are offered, will vary according to the association and its program. One association may appropriately require a monthly report; another may be satisfied with a quarterly report; still another may find that an annual report meets its needs. Whatever the interval, the treasurer should be faithful in rendering financial reports at the specified times. He should also be willing and prepared to submit to questioning by the members on the content of the reports he renders.

(1) Clarity of Financial Reports

It goes without saying that a financial report should be accurate. Equally important, it should explain everything clearly so that everyone concerned can understand it. A financial report that is so obscure that most members cannot see plainly what has been done with their money is worse than useless. Indeed, it invites suspicion, and brings criticism to the treasurer and the governing board. A financial report is really a communication from the person who has handled the association finances, and is directed to members who have not been familiar with them day by day. If a financial report is obscure, it fails as a communication. Every treasurer's report should be crystal clear to those reading it. If technical terms and unusual transactions are involved, they should be explained in lay terms in footnotes. (For further information on footnotes, *see* Part II, I(4).

(2) Paying Attention to Treasurer's Reports

Just as the treasurer has an obligation to give regular reports on the association's financial state, the governing board and other officers have a duty to pay attention to what the treasurer is telling them. If the treasurer urges that certain actions be taken to strengthen the association financially, his colleagues should take him seriously. At the very least, they should consider the matters that the treasurer raises and then, if they wish, they can vote down his proposals.

All too often when a presiding officer calls on the treasurer for a report, group members pay only perfunctory attention to it, then move on to other business that they consider more interesting. An effective treasurer should insist that his proposals for change or for corrective action be placed early on the agenda so there is time to discuss them adequately. If this approach fails at one meeting, he should reach some of his fellow officers before the next meeting to gain allies for a new attempt. And he should prepare and distribute written copies of his proposals with supporting data to make it plain that he means business.

(3)   When the Treasurer Fails to Report

At the start of an administration, it should be made clear to all that the treasurer is expected to give financial reports to the governing board at regular intervals. If he fails to report, the other officers should call on him to do so. This is important because if the association is losing money, or getting into difficulty in any other way, it is the governing board's duty to take the necessary action to improve matters. Corrective steps are not the responsibility of the treasurer alone; the financial state of the association is **everyone's** business.

In a case where the treasurer does not cooperate, for whatever reason, there are several possible courses of action for the president and other officers to follow. One might be for the president to designate an officer who has the best personal rapport with the treasurer to meet with him privately. This officer should try to determine whether the treasurer is incapable of handling the job, or is too lazy to give it the attention it requires, or has some other reason for not reporting. This officer can then report back to the president so the executive body can decide what should be done. A second course might be to find ways to help the treasurer overcome his hesitations and time pressures so that he can produce the financial reports for the rest of his term without loss to the association or embarrassment to anyone. For this it may prove useful to call on a previous treasurer to work in a friendly way with the incumbent treasurer, helping him get on top of the job. A third course, to be used only when other steps fail, would be to replace the treasurer with another member or officer who has given evidence that he will fulfill the duties faithfully. Of course, this should be done with due regard to the feelings of the deposed treasurer.

(C)   The Treasurer as Financial Educator

There are times when an association treasurer meets resistance as he tries to persuade the other officers, or the membership, to take an action that he finds necessary. For example, he might decide that the association should increase its dues, or raise the price for certain activities, or curtail expenditures, or eliminate a costly program. In all such cases he is the bearer of bad news. It is therefore most important that he prepare his arguments so as to be persuasive in a friendly way. And he should emphasize that he is proposing these steps to preserve the financial health of the organization so it can continue to pursue its main objectives.

He should be patient in his explanations, and never lose his composure or become annoyed at those who do not share his outlook. He must remember that he has been in a privileged position permitting him a clearer view of the organization's financial condition than others have had. He cannot expect them to see the situation in the same light that he does. He should be ready to provide graphs and other visual aids that help dramatize the situation, and so bring others around to his point of view.

In especially difficult situations, a treasurer might discuss his proposals with the president, and perhaps a few other officers, in order to enlist their support before a meeting where an unpleasant financial issue must be faced. If he does so, and then goes into the meeting with one or more allies, his position becomes much stronger.

There are also times when the treasurer gains the reputation within an organization of being an obstacle to progress because he argues that it cannot afford actions or programs about which other members are enthusiastic. In fact, it is inevitable that in the minds of some overly-enthusiastic members every treasurer is a cold-hearted Scrooge who really opposes the organization's purposes. There is no way out of this for the conscientious treasurer, especially if he is repeatedly faced with proposals for unrealistic expenditures by members with a Peter Pan approach to financial responsibility. He can only live with the criticism, and trust that in time his colleagues will realize that he was right in protecting the organization from financial folly.

(1)   Accuracy in Reporting Figures

A treasurer should state figures accurately in reports, and avoid any language that suggests he is exaggerating in order to make a point. The figures in a report should speak for themselves. The treasurer cannot afford to lose credibility by stretching or compressing the figures to suit a case he is trying to make. For example, if 47 percent of the members have failed to pay dues, he should report 47 percent—not "half." Or he can report that 188 members are still unpaid out of a membership of 402 (46.77%). If he rounds figures in a report for simplicity, the rounding should be done consistently and fairly so as not to distort the picture. In every association there are enough partisans who manipulate numbers for their own ends. The treasurer should not be among them.

In addition, the treasurer owes it to the members to help them get a true picture of the situation, not a distorted one, by reporting everything relevant. For example, an association account labeled "Annual Meeting" might show a deficit of $1,100.00 at the end of the fiscal year. If the annual meeting account includes $700.00 paid for delayed bills from the previous year's meeting, plus a $500.00 deposit paid to reserve hotel space for the following year's meeting, the report should state these facts. Then association members can see that the present year's meeting really cleared $100.00, rather than sustaining a loss.

(2)   Interpreting the Bank Balance

When an association collects a large amount of money in advance for a program or service for which it must pay later, merely looking at the bank balance by itself can sometimes make the organization appear in better financial health than it really is. For instance, the association may have collected payment for tickets to a luncheon held near the end of the month, but has not paid the caterer's bill until after the monthly bank statement is closed.

When advance collections of this sort materially distort the true financial situation, the treasurer should always accompany any reference to the bank balance with a caution—that a certain amount of the balance represents money that must soon be paid out. As a corollary, should the treasurer report the bank balance without reference to any such accounts payable, he should be asked if there are any bills pending, and their amounts.

(D)   Compensating and Reimbursing the Treasurer

Although most small associations do not compensate any officers for their time and effort, larger organizations with complex affairs may demand so much time from the treasurer that they pay him a modest amount. Whether the treasurer's time, or that of any officer, should be compensated is a policy decision to be made by the organization. In some cases it has been found that a paid treasurer is more responsible than an unpaid one. But this is not universally true. Many individuals subscribe to the volunteer ethic and work devotedly for their associations without payment. So the compensation decision is best decided by the organization and the individual.

Reimbursing the treasurer for expenses he incurs in carrying out his normal duties is a different matter. It is reasonable to let the treasurer bear the expenses of being an ordinary member, such as driving his car to meetings. However, it is a bad practice not to reimburse the treasurer for the out-of-pocket expenses of his office because this discourages other members from serving. The treasurer usually volunteers a great deal of his time, and this is all that should be asked of him. The reimbursement policy should be set forth when the treasurer takes office. This permits him to turn in approved expenses without feeling uncomfortable, and also avoids any unpleasant situations where the treasurer spends money in expectation of reimbursement, and then the organization decides not to reimburse.

The following are some of the items a reimbursement policy should cover:

- Out-of-pocket expenses for supplies and services such as telephone, postage, photocopying, paper, and so forth should be reimbursed.

- If the treasurer does not have access to an adding machine or calculator, the association should buy one and lend it to the treasurer.

- If the treasurer is required to make special trips, mileage reimbursement should be provided. A reasonable mileage rate can be based on the current figure allowed by the IRS for income tax purposes (36 cents in 2003), a figure which the IRS adjusts annually.

Where out-of-town travel is involved, an understanding should be reached in advance regarding meals and lodging. For those organizations that hold conventions, there should be a policy as to whether convention travel expenses are paid. If the treasurer is really needed at the meeting or convention, then it is reasonable that the expenses be reimbursed. If attendance is not essential, but is more of a social event, then reimbursement is discretionary. But in any event the policy should be made known in advance.

Chapter 4. FINANCIAL RECORD-KEEPING

(A)   Checkbook Records
       (1)   Expenditures
       (2)   Deposits

(B)   Documents Supporting Checkbook Entries

(C)   Recording Cash Receipts

(D)   Expenditure Accounts
       (1)   Starting New Accounts

(E)   In-and-Out Accounts

(F)   Duplicate Summary Records for Handy Reference

(G)   Reconciling the Bank Statement
       (1)   Finding Errors
       (2)   "Plugging" an Unbalanced Reconciliation
       (3)   Following Up the Bank Reconciliation

(H)   The Accounting Year

(I)   Margin at Edges of Unbound Record Sheets

CHAPTER 4

Financial Record-Keeping

The association treasurer's most important function is to produce a set of complete and accurate accounting records. Whether this task is fulfilled can often mean the difference between an organization's success or failure, because accurate accounting records—

- Provide a basis for evaluating the organization's past performance
- Provide a basis for future planning and budgeting
- Help prevent loss, embezzlement, or wasteful use of assets
- Provide financial information for potential contributors
- Are necessary for preparation of reports required by the Internal Revenue Service
- Provide data for monitoring compliance with bylaws and grant restrictions
- Furnish information required by banks and other potential lenders.

In short, accounting records provide a foundation for practically every aspect of an organization's management.

Because of the various types and sizes of organizations, and because of the varying degrees of accounting knowledge possessed by treasurers, this chapter presents only the basic principles of record-keeping. More advanced and complicated aspects of the subject, which generally do not apply to small and beginning associations, are discussed in Part II of this book.

(A)   Checkbook Records

The primary record of an organization's expenditures is the checkbook—specifically, the checkbook stubs properly filled out when checks are written and removed. Unless the association pays very few checks in a year, it is advisable to arrange for the bank to provide a large checkbook binder with fillers holding several checks on each page. There should be adequate space on each stub to record the essential information on that payment, and to keep a running balance of funds in the checking account. If the association does not have a suitable checkbook, the treasurer can confer with a bank officer to obtain one designed to meet his needs.

(1)   Expenditures

When the treasurer draws a check on the association account to pay a bill, he should see that the stub provides a clear record of the payment. This means: the amount, the date, the person or company to whom the check was written, purpose of the payment and, when needed, the expenditure account under which it should be listed. Whether the treasurer fills out the stub himself or has it prepared by the office staff, he should make sure that it is both legible and understandable to another person. He should avoid cryptic entries in his private shorthand. In certain cases, he can add an explanatory note if that would be useful to someone else who refers to the checkbook later.

This is a routine checkbook stub with all necessary information:

```
CHECK NO.  1034      $    88.50

DATE:   3/27/xx

TO:  Goldsmith Bros.

FOR:  2/28 Bill – letterhead, envelopes

ACCOUNT:  Stationery


     BALANCE FORWARD    $ 2,437.18
     _____
     DEPOSITS
     _____
     TOTAL THIS CHECK          88.50
     _____
     OTHER DEDUCTIONS
     _____
     BALANCE FORWARD    $ 2,348.68
```

Sometimes it is not obvious which association account is to be charged with an expenditure. Here the cost of mailing envelopes is charged to the Awards Dinner account, rather than to Stationery:

CHECK NO. 1035 $ 27.40

DATE: 3/28/xx

TO: A. B. Smithson Co.

FOR: 2/27 Bill – Mailing envelopes

ACCOUNT: Awards Dinner

BALANCE FORWARD	$ 2,348.68
DEPOSITS	
TOTAL THIS CHECK	27.40
OTHER DEDUCTIONS	
BALANCE FORWARD	$ 2,321.28

A check for an unusual purpose is explained here:

CHECK NO. 1036 $ 75.00

DATE: 4/2/xx

TO: Erwin V. Kayolette

FOR: Refund – dues paid twice in error
    See cash receipts 2/27 and 3/20
ACCOUNT: Dues Received (negative entry)

BALANCE FORWARD	$ 2,321.28
DEPOSITS	
TOTAL THIS CHECK	75.00
OTHER DEDUCTIONS	
BALANCE FORWARD	$ 2,246.28

(2) Deposits

Deposits in the checking account should be recorded on the check stubs when each deposit is made so the treasurer can keep an accurate record of the status of the checking account. The deposit slips, stamped by the bank as receipts, should be kept as a record that the bank acknowledged the deposit and also as a reference in case there is an error in recording the transaction.

If an association handles only a few receipts at a time, and if the checkbook allows room, it may be possible to write on the check stub the source of the money received and deposited (*e.g.*, "John Jones, dues" or "Jane Roe, 2/24 dinner). Or such notations can be made on the deposit slip if space permits. But usually there is not enough space on either. Instead, the facts of each receipt and deposit should be recorded in a cash receipts book when the money reaches the association, and before it is taken to the bank for deposit. This is preferable, because each receipt need be recorded only in the cash receipts book where it can be listed under the proper account. Especially in the case where a dozen people pay cash, rather than checks, at the door of a dinner meeting, it is the only practical way to record their names as paid because there is not room for the names on the deposit slip or a checkbook stub.

Deposits to the association checking account should be specified by date, both to confirm that each deposit was entered in the checkbook and to avoid the mistake of entering a deposit twice. The "other deductions" space on the stub should be used for bank service charges and for dishonored checks that had been deposited and then were returned for lack of sufficient funds.

```
CHECK NO.  1037        $

DATE:   4/25/xx

TO:

FOR:  Deposit of cash receipts

ACCOUNT:  Awards Dinner


        BALANCE FORWARD   $ 2,246.28
        _____
        DEPOSITS                257.90
        _____
        TOTAL THIS CHECK
        _____
        OTHER DEDUCTIONS        10.00
        ___Bank service charge_____
        BALANCE FORWARD   $ 2,494.18
```

(B) Documents Supporting Checkbook Entries

Documents that support the entries on the checkbook stubs should be kept on file until there is no chance they will be useful any longer in analyzing the association's financial condition. Certainly they should be kept for inspection by an audit committee or by an outside accountant who prepares the association's annual financial report. In any event, both bills paid and deposit slips should be retained for four years against a possible audit by the Internal Revenue Service.

Bills that have been paid can be filed in two ways. One method is to file them chronologically when paid, using a clip, folder or staple to hold together all bills paid on a certain date, or in a given week. Should a question arise later about a bill that was paid, the checkbook stub will show the payment date and then the corresponding bill is easily found. Another filing method, which is frequently more troublesome, is to file each paid bill by the name of vendor or payee. This makes it easy to review all the bills from one vendor, such as a printer. But the rare need for such a review usually does not justify all the paper-handling it requires.

Bank deposit slips should be filed chronologically so that it is easy to determine that any deposit marked on the checkbook stubs was indeed made at the bank. With these should be kept any bank slips that notify the association of a bank service charge or of a dishonored check.

(C) Recording Cash Receipts

The treasurer should see that the association keeps an accurate record of all cash received so there is no doubt as to the date on which the money came in, who paid it, and for what purpose. Cash receipts records are best kept safe from damage and loss if they are held in a binder or are recorded in a cash receipts book. Entries should be on lined columnar pages that can be bought at stores that sell business stationery.

All cash receipts should be recorded in ink, not pencil. Each entry should be on its own line in the receipts book and should be dated. The typical cash receipts book should have columns designating the date, amount received, payer's name, and, to the right, several columns marked with the most important revenue sources which the treasurer wants to separate from others. A typical breakdown of sources might include: dues, initiation fees, dinner meeting tickets, association literature, and always "other" or "miscellaneous" for receipts not specified elsewhere.

Every payment received should be recorded twice—once in the cash received column, from which all income recorded on the page can be totaled, and once in an account, or source column, to make it easier to total the money received for that purpose.

Date	Cash Rec'd	Payer	Dues	Initiation	Dinners	Literature	Misc., Other
10/5/xx	65.00	George Long	65.00				
"	22.00	Sally Olde			22.00		
"	14.50	Al Stotler				14.50	
11/6/xx	75.00	Maria Kage	65.00				Club Certificate 10.00

This system allows the treasurer to see quickly how much dues money has come into the treasury, how many dinner tickets have been sold, and the like.

When the last line of the page is reached, each column should be added and the total recorded in pencil (so it can be corrected easily if found wrong). The cash received column total should equal the sum of the separate accounts columns. If it does not, the treasurer should check to see that each entry is correctly made and that each amount received (in the first cash column) is properly entered in one of the account columns on the right. And, of course, the addition of each column bears rechecking. When the page totals are in order, they are carried over to the top of the columns on the next page to help in obtaining a running total later when the end of the new page is reached. By proceeding this way, page by page, it becomes easy at the end of the month (or other accounting period) to obtain the totals for the full month. The cash received column total should equal the total of the separate accounts columns from the first page to the last.

Date	Cash Rec'd	Payer	Dues	Initiation	Dinners	Literature	Misc., Other
10/9	65.00	John Ingles	65.00				
10/10	22.00	Sarah Keller			22.00		
TOTALS	1,196.75		910.00	100.00	88.00	47.25	51.50

Carry forward

Date	Cash Rec'd	Payer	Dues	Initiation	Dinners	Literature	Misc., Other
Carried forward	1,196.75		910.00	100.00	88.00	47.25	51.50

If the association needs the figures, the treasurer can break down the "other" or "miscellaneous receipts" column into its components, using space on the final page of the monthly record to add up these minor accounts. Or he may simply extract the total for one source of income, such as the sale of club certificates, if that is all that is wanted. However, this is possible only if the entries are made with consistent use of terms describing the item or service that is paid for.

(D) Expenditure Accounts

A well-managed association should keep track of how much it is spending during the year under each of a number of headings, rather than wait until the end of the year to determine where the money went. To do this, the treasurer or someone under his direction should take the essential information from the checkbook stubs and reorganize it in a running record of expenditures that provides the answers the organization wants. This is done by preparing an expenditures record with a column for each category that the treasurer wants to isolate, and making entries at regular intervals in much the same manner as is done with cash receipts. If the association wants a record of more spending accounts than the space in the standard account book provides, the treasurer may have to use folded extension pages. Or he might transfer the record of some accounts to another page in the record book.

The decision to account for certain expenditures separately from others depends on whether the separate account category would serve a useful purpose. If it would be useful to know what a given category of expenditures is costing the association, it requires no great effort to account for them separately. But it is a waste of time to cut the association's expenditures into such fine bits that no one really uses the detailed information that results. Exactly which accounts the association officers may want to maintain depends on each association's needs.

The list of accounts kept separately in the expenditures book is called the chart of accounts. Once the chart of accounts is determined, the columns in the expenditures book should be labeled in much the same way as the cash receipts book. There should be columns on the left for the date, the check number, the amount of each check paid, the name of the payee, and then the amount paid should be entered again in the proper column on the right. There should always be a column for "other" to accommodate expenditures that do not fit under one of the listed accounts.

It is usually most productive to use a separate account column for each type of expenditure that requires frequent entries, rather than for those paid just once a month, such as office rent, which can be placed in the "other" column. The separate columns, after all, serve the purpose of helping keep track of frequent expenditures, those of which the total is not clearly known, or those that fluctuate from month to month. For one organization the most frequent entries might be expenses for its weekly luncheon meetings. For another it might be expenses for a periodical. For another, salaries paid to the office staff. The arrangement of the expenditures account book should be based on the convenience of using it. But all checks paid should be entered somewhere in the expenditures record so that it is a complete record of money spent.

Where there are repeated or periodic events under the same heading, such as monthly dinner meetings, the treasurer should designate the exact event to which a check applies. For instance, a check might be written in February to a caterer in payment for the January dinner, and another February check might be an advance payment for the March dinner. These can be separated easily with a notation or a color code. Then the expenditures for one event can be related to the cash receipts for the same event, and the treasurer can determine the gain or loss.

The following illustration shows how entries can be made in an expenditures record with the information taken from the checkbook stubs.

FISCAL 20—EXPENDITURES

DATE	CHECK NO.	AMT. PAID	PAID TO:	STAFF SALARIES	WAGE TAXES PAID	RENT, TELE-PHONE	OFFICERS' EXPENSES	SUPPLIES, STATIONERY	MISC, OTHER
07/10	1892	246.72	M. Voss	246.72					
"	1899	21.15	AT&T			21.15			
"	1902	15.81	Goldsmith Co.					15.81	
07/12	1911	56.20	Marina Bank		56.20				
"	1916	9.50	D. Schultz				9.50		
"	1924	487.20	Scott Co.					(Newsletter printing)	487.20

At the bottom of each page all columns should be added and the total carried over to the top of the following page, as with the cash receipts record. And at the end of each page, the total dollar amount of checks written (in the left-hand column) should equal the total of the separate account columns extended to the right.

The six-column record shown above is suited only to the simplest expenditure pattern of a very small organization. Most associations will need a record with twelve or more columns to permit accounting for all or most of the significant classes of expenditure. If the number of columns on the page still proves insufficient, the "other" column can be extended to a following page where the "other" entries can be made in an additional set of columns.

OTHER	
A.	22.15
B.	435.10
C.	197.16
B.	395.25
C.	136.19

OTHER (from previous page)		
A. Messengers	B. Catering	C. Printing
22.15		
	435.10	
		197.16
	395.25	
		136.19

(1)   Starting New Accounts

When the association starts a new activity in the middle of the fiscal year, or when an old activity divides into two or more parts, the treasurer should ask himself whether it would be useful to start keeping a record of the new activity in mid-year. Generally, if the association would want to know whether the new activity gains or loses money, a new account is needed. At this point, minor amounts already spent in the start-up phase can be disregarded. The starting date of the new account and a note explaining the change should be clearly recorded.

(E)   In-and-Out Accounts

When an association has an activity that generates its own revenue and involves expenditures, such as an annual social affair for which tickets are sold, a separate summary account can be set up to keep track of the money coming in and going out that is directly related to it. This enables the treasurer to determine whether the activity made a profit, suffered a loss, or just broke even. If there are a number of such activities, the treasurer may set up a book of all in-and-out accounts simply to bring the figures together for easy comparison. The details of each check paid in and out are not needed in this accounting because they should be recorded elsewhere in the cash receipts and the expenditures books. Weekly or daily summaries should be sufficient.

Monthly Dinner Meetings

REVENUES			EXPENDITURES	
Jan. 8 Dinner			Jan. 8 Dinner	
12/22-27	Tickets Paid	$ 420	Printing & postage	$ 42
12/29 - 1/3	" "	640	Guest refreshments	72
1/5-8	" "	512	Hotel bill	1,948
1/8	Cash at door	444		
		2,016		2,062
Feb. 12 Dinner			Feb. 12 Dinner	
1/26-31	Tickets paid	316	Printing & postage	36
2/2-7	" "	522		

Sometimes the activity might draw on resources of which the cost is listed in other accounts. Examples are long-distance telephone calls, printing of invitations, or postage directly used to further the activity. Therefore, if the treasurer wants to obtain the full cost of the activity to the association, he should allocate to it a fair share of the cost of such items. Otherwise, they might escape notice, and the association would get a false idea of the full cost of the activity.

It should be noted that all receipts and deposits recorded in an in-and-out account are also recorded in the regular cash receipts record and cash expenditures record, respectively. These latter two records should contain all transactions, even if an in-and-out account is used.

(F)   Duplicate Summary Records for Handy Reference

When the treasurer does not have the records of cash receipts and expenditures in his possession, he may want to have copies or summaries with him for handy reference. This can occur when the records are kept at the association office and the treasurer is there only occasionally. Between such visits he might need to prepare a report using the latest monthly figures for income and outgo. Or he might want to discuss the financial status of the organization with another officer somewhere other than at the association office.

An easy way of obtaining the necessary figures is to prepare a quick income-and-expenditures summary at the end of each month, spelling out the cash receipts total under each heading, with the running total for the fiscal year-to-date. The same can be provided for expenditures—the latest month's total for each expenditures account and the running total for the year. This work can be done by the treasurer or by someone on the staff. Having these figures at hand so he can compare them to the corresponding figures for the previous year enables the treasurer to keep his fingers on the association's financial pulse.

Summary Record, Receipts & Expenditures (First Six Months)

Receipts	Budget For year	Last Month	Total To Date	This Time Last Year
Dues	52,000.	1,000.	49,000.[1]	46,000.
Initiation Fees	1,800.	20.	1,000.	900.
Literature Sales	800.	36.	225.	300.
Other	708.	60.	1,225.	1,010.
	55,308.	1,116.	51,450.	48,210.

Expenditures				
Salaries & Payroll Taxes	30,000.	2,495.	15,100.	13,900.
Rent	5,000.	410.	2,450.	2,450.
Newsletter	10,000.	1,005.	5,840.	4,980.
Stationery & Supplies	500.	30.	280.	300.
Postage	500.	25.	660.	600.
Telephone	2,000.	150.	980.	950.
Officers' Reimbursed Expenses	500.	55.	250.	200.
Insurance [2]	500.	0.	475.	475.
Accounting & Legal Services	1,000.	750.	750.	700.
Federation Dues	1,000.	980.	980.	850.
Awards	500.	0.	0.	0.
Other	3,800.	240.	1,400.	1,300.
	55,300.	6,140.	29,165.	26,705.

In-and-Out Accounts	Receipts		Expenditures	Gain/Loss
Dinners	2,808.		2,910.	(102.)

NOTES:
1. 36 members' dues unpaid to date, 347 are paid.
2. All insurance policies for the year are paid.

(G)   Reconciling the Bank Statement

Reconciling the bank statement and the checkbook means bringing them into agreement by identifying and explaining all differences. Reconciling is essential for a number of reasons, such as:

- Verifying that the cash balance shown in the checkbook is correct
- Locating clerical errors made by either the association or the bank
- Determining the amount of service charges and other fees assessed by the bank
- Uncovering long-outstanding checks that have been lost in the mail or forgotten by payees
- Discouraging embezzlement

Reconciling, in other words, prevents misinformation in the organization's records about the cash balance and also helps prevent actual cash losses. The bank statement should be reconciled monthly, without fail. Attempting a multi-month catch-up reconciliation can be a nightmare. Experienced accountants know that it is easier to do three separate monthly reconciliations than one three-month reconciliation. Besides, delaying the reconciliation means that the correction of errors is also delayed, creating the potential for even further damage.

Since the checkbook balance and the amount on the bank statement seldom agree, the process of reconciliation is used to determine the nature of the differences and whether they are proper. Most differences fall into three categories:

Outstanding checks. These are checks that have been written and recorded in the organization's books but are not shown on the bank statement. Usually this time lag is due to the mails and the check clearing system, plus any time that the payee holds the check before cashing it. The dollar amount of outstanding checks is determined by taking the canceled checks returned with the bank statement, comparing the amounts and check numbers to those in the checkbook, marking each check stub with an "x" or "✓" where the canceled check is returned, and then adding up the check stubs not so marked.

Deposits in transit. These are deposits recorded on the association's books but not shown on the bank statement. Generally these are deposits mailed in the last few days before receipt of the bank statement, and which are not entered in the statement because of the time required for processing and mailing. The amount of deposits in transit is determined by taking the deposit tickets returned with the bank statement, locating the corresponding deposits in the checkbook, marking the check stub deposit entry with an "x" or "✓", and then adding up the check stub deposit entries which have not been so marked.

Miscellaneous items. These may be various bank charges (minus) or the month's interest (plus) shown on the bank statement but not on the association books. Charges commonly include those for account maintenance, check printing, lockboxes, dishonored checks, and overdrafts. These may be found in the top line of the bank statement or in the body of the bank statement where check amounts are listed. In the latter situation the charge will be indicated either by an abbreviated notation beside the amount, or by a special bank ticket included in the stack of canceled checks and deposit tickets. All miscellaneous items in this category should then be recorded in the organization's books and in the checkbook.

Once these three amounts have been determined, the reconciliation form can be filled in. The back side of most bank statements includes such a form, or one similar to that below may be used:

BANK STATEMENT closing balance	$
ADD: total deposits in transit	+
Subtotal	
SUBTRACT: total outstanding checks	-
TOTAL	$
CHECKBOOK balance	$
ADD: interest	+
Subtotal	
SUBTRACT: bank charges	-
total dishonored checks	-
TOTAL	$

If all entries are made correctly, the above two "TOTAL" figures for the bank statement and the checkbook should agree, taking into account the adjustments discussed above. If not, an error has been made somewhere.

(1)   Finding Errors

When the first attempt at reconciling the bank statement fails, many people have a tendency to blame the bank. But in ninety-nine cases out of a hundred the discrepancy is due to an error by the bank customer. The difference between the bank statement and the association records could be due to one or a combination of the following factors:

- Checks written or bank deposits made which were not recorded in the checkbook. This type of error should have been discovered when the outstanding checks and deposits in transit were figured, in the form of a canceled check or deposit ticket for which no entry in the checkbook could be found.

- Check or deposit amounts recorded in the checkbook but in the wrong amount. Again, this type of error should have been discovered when outstanding checks and deposits in transit were figured, provided the amounts on the canceled checks and deposit tickets were compared carefully to the amounts on the check stubs.

- Addition or subtraction errors in the checkbook. Such an error in arithmetic is indicated if the entries for checks written and deposits are the same on the checkbook stubs as those listed in the bank statement, yet the account balances are different. In this case, the checkbook entries should be recalculated.

- Errors in the reconciliation process. This could occur in one of the six basic steps: identifying outstanding checks, adding up outstanding checks, identifying deposits in transit, adding up deposits in transit, identifying miscellaneous items, and adding up miscellaneous items. These steps should be repeated. If the reconciliation is still off after checking for the types of errors listed above, the search technique might be changed to the methods described in Part II, H, Finding Errors.

(2)   "Plugging" an Unbalanced Reconciliation

Should a treasurer ever "plug" an unbalanced reconciliation to make it come out in balance—or, at least, to appear that way? This can be done by charging the difference to miscellaneous income or expense. The answer is a matter of opinion. Some lazy bookkeepers are always plugging their records, whereas others religiously refuse to do so and will spend hours looking for a two-cent difference. There is a reasonable approach between these two.

Plugging by even a penny should be distasteful because it means that there is an error somewhere. But there are occasions when the difference is so small that it is impractical to spend a long time looking for it. After making a good-faith effort to balance the reconciliation, it is usually acceptable for a treasurer to hold his nose and make an infrequent, small plug. But what is "small?" If the treasurer would be concerned about losing that amount of cash, it is not small enough. If the difference is no more than a couple of dollars, say, and the association would not be concerned about losing that amount of cash, then it is within plugging range. If in doubt, search it out.

One requirement when plugging: Always clearly label the plug, perhaps calling it an "unlocated difference." Never hide the amount in another category because occasionally it is necessary to know the amount of the plug when preparing future records.

(3)   Following Up the Bank Reconciliation

Completing the reconciliation does not complete the task; a reconciliation is not an end in itself but a means to better cash management. Now the differences (or "reconciling items") between the checkbook and the bank statement must be considered for propriety and corrective action, if necessary. Specific differences due to bank errors should be reported to the bank, of course. Checks which have been outstanding for sixty days or longer should also be looked at. Although some payees such as government agencies are slow in cashing checks, after two or three months it is probable that the check has been lost and will never be cashed. In such a situation the organization has two basic options:

- Make contact with the payee and find out what should be done. If a replacement check is issued, the bank should be notified to stop payment on the old check.

- If the organization would prefer not to make another payment, for whatever reason, payment on the check can be stopped, or alternatively, nothing at all need be done. In this case, the check will continue to be outstanding on future reconciliations.

Deposits in transit should also be examined to see if any are in transit too long. If a deposit is mailed more than three days before the bank statement date but is not shown on the statement, something is wrong. The bank should be called to make sure the deposit has not been lost. Should the time lag between mailing deposits and receiving credit for them become serious, or if there is a record of deposits going astray in the mail, the association should consider making deposits in person rather than using the mails.

If, during reconciliation, the treasurer should observe that one or more people make a habit of paying the association with checks that are returned for lack of sufficient funds, he should consider taking corrective action. In such a case, it is politic for him to discuss the matter confidentially with the president or another officer so that if action is taken he has support from a responsible source.

(H)   The Accounting Year

All organizations must use an annual accounting period. This provides the officers and members with a fixed length of time for measuring financial results, and is also required for reporting to the Internal Revenue Service. Many organizations use the calendar year because this is most familiar and coincides with bank reporting of interest income, payroll reporting for employee W-2s, and a variety of other clerical items handled on a December 31 year-end.

However, a new organization may use the last day of any month for its year-end, giving it twelve possibilities to choose from. There are several reasons why an organization might want to select a fiscal year rather than the calendar year. If the organization's operation is seasonal, a year-end during a slack period is often used to make the closing of books easier because activities and financial transactions will be at a lower level. For instance, a club with an active program from September into late spring might want to use a June 30 year-end because usually this would be the quiet time to close the books. This would also be the case with a student organization, such as a fraternity, where the financial year should coincide with the academic year.

Although generally the last day of a month must be used for the year-end, there is one exception—the 52/53-week year. Here the year-end always falls on the same day of the week (always ending on Saturday, for instance). This causes the year to be either 52 or 53 weeks long, rather than 365 days. Few organizations use the 52/53-week year, but it has advantages in certain special situations. If the organization's payroll period is weekly or biweekly, it may be convenient to have the year-end always coincide with the end of the payroll period, thereby avoiding the problem of splitting payroll at year-end. Or if the association involves a shop that must be closed for a day to count inventory at year-end, a 52/53-week year can be used to have the year-end always fall on a Saturday or Sunday when the shop would have been closed anyway. Thus, the sales for a regular business day are not lost.

An IRS requirement for a 52/53-week year is that once a particular weekday is chosen (Saturday, for instance), the year-end must occur on the last such weekday in a chosen month, or on the <u>closest</u> such weekday to the last day of the chosen month. Thus, if Saturday were selected as the key weekday and June as the key month, the year-end would always fall on either the last Saturday in June, or on the Saturday that falls nearest to June 30—which might be as late as July 3rd. (The organization must consistently use either the last Saturday or the nearest Saturday—it may not switch back and forth.)

In short, the new organization may choose any year-end consistent with the above rules. The best year-end is found by answering these two questions:

- What year-end will make the financial data most meaningful?

- What year-end will be easiest for the treasurer and the organization?

NOTE: The above discussion pertains primarily to non-profit tax-exempt organizations. A for-profit <u>partnership</u>, such as an investment club, must generally use a calendar year.

A new organization signifies its choice of a year-end to the IRS by filing a tax return (IRS Form 990 for most tax-exempt organizations) for the period beginning with the organization's first day of operation and running to the chosen year-end. This is known as a "short period" because it is rarely a full year. In addition to the tax return, a tax return extension form (usually IRS Form 8868) will establish the year-end. Once established, the year-end may be difficult to change; therefore this fact should be kept in mind whenever the first tax return or extension form is filed. On the other hand, although the application for a federal identification number and the application for exempt status (*see*, Part II, B) request the anticipated year-end, answers on these forms do not bind the organization to this year-end and it may be changed. Only a tax return or extension form definitely fixes the year-end.

To repeat: The new organization has great freedom in choosing its accounting year, but there is no great freedom to change the year once it is established. For further information on changing the year, refer to Part II, L.

(I)   Margin at Edges of Unbound Record Sheets

Sometimes the treasurer and office staff of a new association will keep financial records on loose accounting sheets rather than in bound ledger books. When this is done, those keeping the records should avoid recording essential information, especially totals of columns and lines, on the extreme outer edges of the sheets. Repeated handling and filing can make hand-written figures on the outer edges difficult to read, or can destroy them completely. Therefore, at least a half-inch margin should be left unused on all four edges of unbound sheets of this kind. Better still, keep all financial records in binders that protect the edges of each page.

Chapter 5. THE TREASURER AS BUSINESS MANAGER

(A)   Using a Budget

(B)   Internal Controls
- (1)   The Philosophy of Internal Controls
- (2)   Budget Analysis
- (3)   Separation of Duties
- (4)   Controls Over Cash Receipts
- (5)   Handling Cash Donations
- (6)   Controls Over Cash Disbursements
- (7)   Control Over Petty Cash
- (8)   Prenumbered Documents
- (9)   The Annual Audit
- (10)   Fidelity Bonds
- (11)   Safeguarding Cash in a Public Place
- (12)   Prompt Depositing of Checks Received

(C)   Monitoring Financial Trends
- (1)   Reimbursement of Expenses
- (2)   Controlling Free Admissions and Giveaways
- (3)   Fellowship Expenses
- (4)   Controlling the Office Work Load
- (5)   Employee Salaries and Benefits
- (6)   Expected Income

(D)   Investing Idle Cash

(E)   Custody of Books and Records
- (1)   Treasury Filing System
- (2)   Action Guides to the Files
- (3)   Cleaning the Files and Document Retention

CHAPTER 5

The Treasurer as Business Manager

(A)   Using a Budget

One of the treasurer's most important functions is managing the budget. Some treasurers will point out that their association does not have a budget; our response is that it should. If the association refuses to adopt a budget, then possibly the treasurer should prepare an unofficial one on his own. A budget is merely a statement or plan of expected income and expenditures over the coming time period. It offers these advantages:

- It helps determine what future programs the association can afford and avoids spending on impulse.

- It helps the governing board to plan since it shows what is expected financially.

- Once programs are under way, it helps control costs because the officers and committees have an incentive to reach stated goals. If they do not meet the goals, there may be criticism.

- By providing reimbursement for officers' expenses, it avoids the bad practice of having officers pay their own expenses, and thus be discouraged from serving because of the financial drain.

- It avoids having to submit each separate expenditure for approval by the membership and wasting everyone's time in discussion of petty amounts. Instead, the total annual expenditures can be approved at one meeting.

- It helps detect a fraud, since often that would appear as a deviation from expected receipts and expenditures.

- It points out problem areas that require additional attention—if budget goals are not met.

This all makes budgets look extremely valuable, and indeed they are. However, there are a few problems to watch out for, but they result from laxity in implementing the budget rather than shortcomings of the budget concept itself.

"Budgetitis" may set in. This occurs when no attempt is made to cut waste as long as expenses do not exceed the budget. The result is more expenses than necessary—and waste is never good, regardless of whether expenses are above or below the budget. In some organizations budgetitis can border on dishonesty where wasteful expenditures are <u>intentionally</u> made at year-end just to use up the full budgeted amount. This happens sometimes when the spender fears that his budget for next year will be reduced if expenditures for the current year are below budget.

Another product of shallow thinking is automatic approval in the current year for <u>at least</u> the prior year's budgeted amount. In this situation, programs already started do not need to be justified, and it is presumed that they should be continued or even expanded. As a result, some obsolete and wasteful programs continue indefinitely. The cure for this is popularly called "zero-based budgeting," under which all programs in the budget-making process start out with zero balances each year. All proposed expenses of the program must then be examined and justified—not just the increase over the previous year.

Another problem with budgeting is that it may hamper flexibility to meet an unexpected opportunity during the year. Some may argue that "since it isn't provided for in the budget," a new activity should not be undertaken. Of course, one of the reasons for a budget is to discourage impulsive spending. But if an unexpected and truly deserving opportunity does arise, the treasurer or another officer should take the initiative to propose the necessary action despite the budget.

With the above points in mind, the treasurer should follow these steps in preparing the budget:

- <u>Select the budget period</u>. Almost always this is a year, but shorter periods such as a month or a quarter may be used as well. For a few programs there may be budgets for a longer period, such as two or even five years, in addition to an annual one. However, periods other than a year are generally supplements to the annual budget, not replacements for it.

- <u>Determine the budget categories, or accounts</u>. Probably the best system is to list all the income and expense accounts and use these as the budget categories. If there are just too many accounts, then combine them into meaningful groups. However, do not make the mistake of combining to the point that only a few broad, bland categories remain. Everyone has seen reports of large organizations which list only "Contributions," "Other Income," "Program Expenses," or "Administrative Expenses." This type of condensation makes a budget almost useless. It is better to err on the side of too much detail rather than too little. In addition, there should be categories for revenue as well as expenses. Some organizations have budgets for expenditures only. In this case the organization cannot tell whether revenue-raising efforts have been effective or whether someone is pocketing receipts. Equally important, many expenses fluctuate with revenues (such as the cost of literature or club insignia for sale) and analyzing revenues is necessary to determine whether such expenditures have exceeded the proper percentage of income.

■ <u>Determine the budget amounts for each category</u>. Obviously there is no mechanical procedure that produces these figures. Instead, good budgets are the product of common sense and judgment after taking into account all the circumstances, such as:

✓ The previous year's actual results and budget (if any). Remember the zero-based concept and watch out for unnecessary or excessive programs.

✓ The effect any new programs may have on those continued from the previous year.

✓ Consistency within the budget, which requires setting related accounts in the proper proportion to each other. For example, if salaries are to be increased, payroll taxes should be raised in the right proportion.

✓ The current inflation rate.

After all these steps have been taken, the budget is ready for approval by the appropriate body. In small organizations the entire membership may vote on it; in others, approval may be by a special committee or by the president. Later in the year any expenditures in excess of the budget may require special approval.

For activities that involve both income and expenditures, such as monthly dinner meetings for which tickets are bought, budgeting is often not realistic. An organization cannot predict at the start of the year what the attendance will be at such affairs because the members' interest in each program may vary widely. Therefore, it is useful to set a general policy, such as aiming to break even on the year's dinner meetings, or to realize a modest profit on them. Then periodic reports by the treasurer should show how such an in-and-out activity is contributing toward the established goal.

An Annual Budget			LAST YEAR (ACTUAL)
Projected Revenues and Expenditures for the Fiscal Year			
REVENUES:			
dues	20,000		19,150
initiation fees	1,000		980
application fees	200		210
sales of literature	500		445
other	100		150
	21,800		20,935
EXPENDITURES:			
salaries and payroll taxes		13,000	12,750
rent		2,400	2,360
Newsletter		3,000	3,100
telephone		400	395
postage		600	585
stationery & supplies		300	310
accounting & legal services		1,000	990
officers' reimbursed expenses		150	145
insurance		200	210
other		200	180
		21,250	21,025
IN-AND-OUT ACCOUNTS:			
dinner meetings (breakeven)			- 110
annual conference	+ 300		+ 320
hospital insurance program (breakeven)			- 10
Christmas party	+ 200		+ 280
other			0
	22,300	21,250	+ 390 (surplus)

Once the budget is approved, the treasurer should not put it aside and forget about it until the end of the year. He should monitor actual results throughout the year in comparison with the budget, using an appropriate percentage in each account to reflect the months that have passed. The time to cut waste is when it is incurred—not at the end of the year. It follows also that if a budget category appears to be insufficient, the best course of action is to notify the president or the executive board as soon as possible. It is the treasurer's job to be alert to such situations and to put the responsibility for corrective action where it belongs. This is much better than a treasurer's letting things go and then trying to defend himself against criticism months later.

(B) Internal Controls

One of the primary accounting concerns of a small organization is preventing misappropriation of its funds by those to whom it is entrusted—or embezzlement, in legal terms. This concern should not be a paranoia that overshadows other important objectives, because the main purpose of the association is not to protect its funds but to perform services for members or the community. On the other hand, embezzlement is a potential problem that should not be overlooked. It is difficult for the association to operate if a significant part of its funds are siphoned off by an embezzler. The intangible damage can be equally great—distrust, disruption and adverse publicity. People do not want to contribute to an organization whose money is mishandled. Not only that, but a great deal of valuable time of the officers can be spent investigating a loss rather than carrying out the organization's function.

There are a number of reasons why a small nonprofit organization is more susceptible to fraud than an ordinary business:

- Generally there is less supervision of money matters. Officers usually are either part-time volunteers with limited time to supervise, or they are untrained in business matters—or both.

- Those handling the money are more likely to have an unbusinesslike attitude—meaning that the temptation is greater to borrow organization funds for personal use.

- The treasurer's work is sometimes viewed as a necessary evil to be avoided by everyone except the treasurer. Often no questions are asked. If they are, any explanation is automatically accepted, because if the treasurer views the questioning as harassment, he might resign, leaving the unwelcome task to someone else.

For these reasons, every treasurer and every association should pay attention to internal controls. The discussion that follows will help the officers of an association control the treasurer, and will help the treasurer control other people, including the office staff and other members. And even for the honest treasurer with no one working under him, the implementation of internal controls should be considered to protect the organization from a future treasurer who may not be so honest. While the emphasis is on preventing dishonesty, most of this section is equally applicable to preventing honest errors by the financial officer. Such errors are far more common and can be almost as damaging as an embezzlement. Therefore, whenever fraud prevention is referred to, error prevention is also implied.

(1)   The Philosophy of Internal Controls

How can embezzlement (or errors) be prevented? There is no foolproof way regardless of how many precautions are taken. However, an organization can make the possibility of <u>significant</u> embezzlement extremely unlikely. The steps to be taken depend on the circumstances of each organization—its nature, members and size. Some steps will be applicable to even the smallest and simplest organization; others will be applicable only in certain circumstances.

Few methods directly prevent fraud before it happens. An exception would be countersigning of checks or some similar device to require approval before assets of the organization are released. Instead, most methods are designed to detect fraud after it happens. Running an operation tightly enough to prevent any fraud from starting would be a nightmare, because every transaction, both incoming and outgoing, would have to be closely supervised. Few would voluntarily serve as treasurer in such a situation. Detecting fraud after it starts is usually sufficient, since most embezzlements start small and stretch over a long period. Early detection will therefore prevent serious losses. Furthermore, the probability of detection, while not actually making the start of fraud impossible, will usually be an effective deterrent since the potential white-collar criminal in an association does not want to risk public embarrassment and a possible jail sentence.

Internal controls may cause some people to say indignantly: "Don't you trust me?" Frankly, the answer should be, "Not completely." Of course, this should never be said for reasons of tact. An individual is trusted enough to be the custodian of the organization's property, which should be considered a compliment. However, no person should be trusted enough to have an unsupervised, unrestricted free hand with the organization's assets. The others cannot know the person that well.

The proper response in this situation should be one or both of these:

- "We trust you, but we don't know who future treasurers will be. If we drop the controls for you, how will we handle future treasurers?"

- "Besides, internal controls are needed to catch honest errors. We know you're honest, but anybody can make a mistake. Something might be overlooked or put in the wrong account."

So much for the reasons why internal controls are important. The following pages describe some internal control steps that every organization should consider.

(2)   Budget Analysis

A properly used budget is not only the best way to prevent significant fraud, but is also a vital management tool. Properly comparing the budget to actual results is one way in which fraud can be detected.

Too often, though, the comparison is made in a mechanical manner, with the result of greatly reduced effectiveness. Significant differences may be noted, but explanations are too often accepted automatically rather than being critically considered. Where there is no difference, no questions are raised at all under this erroneous approach.

Making a proper comparison means that the relationship between items in the actual results is considered, in addition to differences between the actual results and the budget. This will generally prevent an embezzler from getting away with a smooth-sounding, but false, explanation. For instance, a bookkeeper may claim that office supplies have exceeded budget because of additional mailings of publications. If this is true, then postage expense should be up as well, along with revenue from the sale of publications. If both of these accounts have not changed by an appropriate amount, a further investigation should be made.

The point is that unexpected results in one account may be accompanied by unexpected results in one or more other accounts. However, one should not concentrate exclusively on accounts that are over budget, although these naturally should receive extra attention. Accounts that are equal to or below budget should also be analyzed. A smart embezzler would hide his defalcations in an account that was otherwise low. Thus, do not pass over the salaries expense account merely because it is 10 percent less than budget. If one-third of the employees have left the payroll, perhaps the account balance should be significantly lower than it is.

Intelligent budget analysis is the most important internal control step that an organization can take. It is the best way of detecting a large fraud. Compared to other internal control procedures, the time and training required to perform budget analysis are relatively modest.

But detecting fraud is not the only benefit, or even the primary one. The biggest payoff comes from added management efficiency. Perhaps only a small percentage of all organizations experience significant fraud, but almost all organizations suffer from inefficiency to a greater or lesser degree. After all, there is no such thing as a perfect operation. And because of the vital management benefits of a budget, budget analysis is an internal control step that can be implemented without someone's getting the notion that he is not trusted.

If for some reason an organization does not have a budget, the treasurer can at least compare this year's actual results to last year's results. While not as effective as a careful budget analysis, this technique will help uncover major irregularities.

(3)   Separation of Duties

The concept underlying most of the remaining internal control steps is that of separation of duties. Ideally, the person who controls the records should not be the person who controls the assets themselves. Then, periodically, the records should be compared to the actual assets. If these steps are taken, a loss of assets would be discovered because the records would show more, and an error in the records would be uncovered because the actual assets would not agree with the records.

This assumes, of course, that there is no collusion between the record-keeper and the asset-keeper. So long as the two are not closely related and each is properly screened for trustworthiness, this is a reasonable assumption. Almost all frauds are the work of a lone embezzler. There are a few exceptions, of course, but no system of controls is foolproof. The minimal risk of sophisticated, multi-person fraud is unavoidable in an imperfect world. Besides, a proper budget analysis should uncover any large losses.

(4)   Controls Over Cash Receipts

Cash is usually a small organization's most important asset. In the case of cash, the person who controls the records is the one who handles the cash journals. The person who controls the asset itself is the one who signs the checks or receives incoming funds. So long as these duties are separated and the records are periodically compared to the actual cash balance through a bank reconciliation performed by an independent person, a fraud will usually be uncovered, assuming there is no collusion and that one person does not trick the other.

Here is the way these functions can be properly separated. With regard to incoming cash, one person should be designated to open the mail and list any checks received by name and amount. This person should then deposit the checks. Afterwards, the list is turned over to another person who posts the receipts to the appropriate accounts in the cash receipts record book.

It is true that the mail opener could steal incoming checks. Even though the check is made out to the organization, an individual can sometimes manage to open a new account in the organization's name at another bank with himself as the authorized check signer. Whenever he needs money, the embezzler then simply writes a check to himself. For that matter, a check made out to the association can often be deposited directly into a personal account, without the need for a phony account in the organization's name. The embezzler simply signs the association's name on the back of the check and deposits it in his account. So long as the endorsement does not contain the words, "For deposit only," most bank tellers will not raise any questions.

However, such a stolen check will generally be detected if record-keeping duties are segregated. If the check is a payment for membership dues, the member will not receive proper credit for the payment and will complain when sent a statement later. If the check is a contribution, successful theft may be a bit easier if the donor does not expect an acknowledgment. However, the IRS now requires an acknowledgment for contributions of $250.00 or more (*see* Chapter 6(G)), and small contributions may be voluntarily acknowledged when made or via an annual statement. Providing this documentation to donors helps counteract the risk of theft since donors may complain if there is a discrepancy between their contributions and the reported amount. An acknowledgment or statement is also a good idea from a fund-raising standpoint since it lets donors know they are appreciated, and also jogs their memory to send a further contribution. Again, the mail opener should not be involved in sending these statements to members or donors, or in keeping the records from which these statements are prepared.

One should not be hasty and say that the organization is too small for this separation of duties. A secretary or receptionist can open the mail, list the checks and make the deposit. If there simply is not a person to do this, a bank lockbox can be used. Then members and donors can be instructed to send their payments to a bank, which prepares a listing of deposits and credits them to the organization's checking account a day or two sooner than would otherwise be the case. Also, the bank would presumably make good any loss caused by the embezzlement of a bank employee.

If duties are not segregated, here are some of the things that can happen to cash receipts:

- Lapping. This is a classic form of fraud in which a person steals an incoming check and then uses a future incoming check to cover the missing one, a still future check to cover the first substitute, and so on *ad infinitum*. For instance, the person steals a check for a dinner ticket, but has the ticket sent to the member anyway to prevent any complaint. Cash in the bank is now short, though, so to correct this, another member's check is used to replace the first one. Then another check replaces the second one. The same thing can be done with contributions or payments for any other purpose. This problem is greatest, of course, when the person handling the incoming checks also keeps the books. Conceivably, it could also be done even if someone else keeps the books, provided the lapping is done on the list of deposits by the person opening the mail. In this situation, the person begins by removing a check and makes no mention of it on the deposit list. The next day, an incoming check for the same amount is listed as being from the person who sent the stolen check. Soon another check is shown as being from the person who sent the first substitute check, and so forth.

Probably the best way to detect this deposit list fraud before it gets serious is to have an independent person periodically compare the incoming checks to the deposit list on a surprise basis. Once every month or two, an officer should generously "offer" to take the deposit to the bank after the mail opener has prepared the deposit list. When he can do it discreetly, the officer should then compare the checks to the deposit list. If they do not agree, lapping may be in process. The same may be true if the mail opener refuses the officer's repeated offers to help. A certified public accountant probably should be called in at this point. The bank's microfilm copies of prior deposit slips and incoming checks can be used to resolve the issue.

Another good way to combat lapping is by insisting that the mail opener take a week or two of vacation each year. This will temporarily stop the lapping treadmill and allow a significant loss to surface.

- The bad-debt writeoff. This is most likely to occur when an association makes sales to outsiders who are not members. If the mail opener is allowed to keep the accounts receivable records of such outside customers, a payment may be stolen. Then, to keep the customer from complaining if he is billed again, the embezzler may write off the receivable amount to bad debts expense so that customer will not be billed. This problem can be avoided by having all bad debt writeoffs approved by an independent person. This is not a demeaning requirement since giving up collection efforts is a management decision as opposed to an accounting one.

- Kiting. This occurs where the organization has more than one bank account and "float" between the accounts is used to cover up a cash shortage. Suppose an embezzler steals $1,000.00 from one account. To cover up this shortage, a check for $1,000.00 is written on the other account and deposited in the first account. Now the first account has been restored to the proper balance. In the second account, a mere transfer to the first account may not seem suspicious to a casual observer.

When preparing the bank reconciliation, the embezzler will usually show the $1,000.00 as a deposit-in-transit on the first account, but not show the $1,000.00 as an outstanding check on the second account. This "boosts" the combined bank balances by $1,000.00 more than really exists and covers up the shortage when financial statements are prepared.

Unless the embezzler repays the funds, though, the $1,000.00 float will never go away and will appear on all future bank reconciliations. Additional thefts will make the float cumulatively larger, and therefore more conspicuous on bank reconciliations.

Where the organization has more than one bank account, kiting may be detected by scanning each bank reconciliation for a deposit-in-transit from the other account. If there is none, there is probably no kiting. If there is such a deposit-in-transit, though, an outstanding check for the same amount should be shown on the bank statement for the other account. If no outstanding check is shown, you may have a kiting situation.

(5)   Handling Cash Donations

Cash donations may often be given in person—the most common example being a church where the offering plate is passed around. To avoid pilferage, two persons can count the cash. Alternatively, donors can put their offering in envelopes with the amount written on the outside. One person can then record the amounts before handing the unopened envelopes over to another person for deposit. Donors would receive an annual statement of contributions and some might complain if they were not credited with the full amount. If donations are received at a central point, such as a booth at a fair, control can be achieved by giving each donor a prenumbered receipt, with a carbon copy retained by the organization. The total of the prenumbered receipts should equal the cash on hand.

(6)   Controls Over Cash Disbursements

Organizations tend to be more sensitive about fraud in the area of disbursements than receipts. In reality, though, disbursements are safer from fraud than receipts. It is unlikely that anyone would be brazen enough to write a check to himself, although this has happened, of course.

If record-keeping and check-writing duties are not segregated, the chances of embezzlement are greatest. The individual then has the ability to conceal the fraud by misclassifying the fraudulent check. The check, whether made out to himself, to a phony company, or for a personal expense, may be entered in the books under office supplies, miscellaneous expense, travel or some other account that appears innocent. Where duties cannot be segregated, budget analysis can help detect any sizable misclassifications.

Some organizations require that checks be signed by two people (cosigned) to minimize the chances of fraud. There are advantages and disadvantages to this approach. Obviously, a person will be less likely to write a fraudulent check if another person will also be signing it. However, many cosigners will quickly sign checks with little or no thought about it. Some may even sign a number of blank checks in advance and never see the check filled out. On the other hand, the cosigning requirement can be quite a burden when the cosigner is out of town or otherwise not available. As a partial solution to this difficulty, some organizations may allow any officer to cosign. To eliminate the cosigning inconvenience for small items, organizations may also provide that only checks over a certain amount (such as $500.00) need to be cosigned. An embezzler, though, could get around this requirement by writing a number of checks for $499.00 each rather than one large check. The main point about cosigning is that while it can help prevent fraud, it is far from foolproof and the organization should not be lulled into a false sense of security. Other internal control steps, such as segregation of duties, should still be used whenever possible.

Even if duties are segregated, however, there is still the possibility of fraud. One kind of fraud is through writing checks to a phony company. The expenditure may even be supported by phony invoices, which can be obtained through a stationery store. To minimize this possibility, invoices should be reviewed twice. If checks are cosigned, each signer can review them. If there is just one check signer, he can approve the invoice when he signs the check, and the keeper of the cash expenditures record book can review it again when recording the transaction (which can be after the check is issued). Without dual review, one person could slip the phony invoice through. In a small organization, presumably both individuals are familiar enough with the operation to know who is really doing business with it. Budget analysis is an additional safeguard here.

A similar, though less obvious, problem arises when one of the officers or office staff causes the organization to do business with a company in which he has an ownership interest. If the relationship is fair and arm's-length, there is no harm. However, prices may be inflated or unnecessary items ordered. Dual review of invoices, together with a knowledge of the organization's needs, the outside activities of its employees, and careful budget analysis are the best ways to prevent serious abuses here.

Still another form of fraud is for an individual to write checks for his personal expenses. Since the check is not made out to himself, the fraud may not be immediately obvious. For instance, if the person uses considerable amounts of stationery at his office or home, the club check would be made out to the stationery supplies store. This type of fraud can also usually be stopped by dual review of supporting invoices.

A spectacular but highly unusual form of fraud occurs when the treasurer, instead of embezzling over a long period of time, steals a huge amount at once and then disappears. This risk is minimal where the treasurer is an established member of the community, but occasionally even pillars of society go berserk. For instance, consider the following news article from the February 19, 1982 issue of *The New York Times*:

CHURCH MISSING $165,000, TREASURER VANISHES

The 59-year-old treasurer of a Rockland County Episcopal church, who had been a respected member of his century-old congregation for 27 years, has absconded with at least $165,000, and possibly as much as $300,000, in church funds, the Rockland County District Attorney said yesterday.

The suspect...vanished on Jan. 30 after the rector and several directors of Christ Church of Ramapo asked him for an explanation of discrepancies in the accounts of the church's funds, according to District Attorney Kenneth Gribetz.

A subsequent check of church bank accounts and investments indicated that [he] apparently had systematically put church funds into bank accounts and liquid money-market funds in his own name in upstate New York, Mr. Gribetz said. The money in the account disappeared when [he] vanished.

"Our people are shocked, they just feel ill," the church rector, the Rev. John A. Andrews, said last night. "Why this man, of all people? It is totally out of the context of everything he portrayed to people. He was upstanding and well-liked by many."

A small amount of caution can prevent such catastrophic frauds. First, a requirement that checks be cosigned should be an effective obstacle. Even a careless cosigner would question a huge check made out to the treasurer. But this defense is lost if the cosigner presigns some blank checks.

If, for reasons of convenience, an association requires only one signature, it can still avoid the huge, one-shot theft. This is done by keeping the checking account balance low. The amount should be limited to that needed for routine operations. Excess amounts should go into some kind of investment that requires dual signatures for withdrawal. Then even if the treasurer should still clean out the checking account and disappear, the loss would be limited. The invested funds (stocks, bonds, savings accounts, certificates of deposit, money market funds, trust management funds) would not be stolen—at least not without the collusion of the other signer. This should cause little inconvenience since the checks need only one signature, and withdrawals of invested funds would be infrequent. In addition to preventing fraud, this technique is also good cash management since unneeded cash balances will earn investment income instead of sitting idly in a checking account.

(7)   Control Over Petty Cash

Many organizations have a petty cash fund and want to know how to control it. Actually, the best control is simply not to have such a fund. However, it is convenient to have a small amount of cash available for such things as payments for postage due, United Parcel Service charges when a package is picked up at the office door, or taxi fare for a member of the office staff.

If a decision is made to have a petty cash fund, a typical size for a small organization is fifty dollars. Some larger organizations have bigger funds, but the larger balance is often unnecessary, and payments of large amounts should be made by check. To determine how large a petty cash fund should be, the treasurer should calculate the unavoidable cash needs of the association office over a reasonable period, which should not exceed one month. Then the figure should be rounded off so it is easy to remember. Let us say it is fifty dollars for purpose of illustration.

To withdraw funds from petty cash, a signed receipt, IOU, or some other form of documentation must be put in the cash box, giving name, date and purpose of the withdrawal. The amount of cash in the box, plus the amount of all receipts, should equal fifty dollars at all times, without exception. When cash runs low, a replenishment is made by check to bring cash back up to fifty dollars—no more and no less. Any receipts in the box should now be removed and stored elsewhere to avoid confusion. The receipts should be reviewed at this time to see that the expenses are legitimate. Every time cash is replenished, the receipts should be cleaned out in this way.

If these procedures are followed, there should be no problems with petty cash, so long as the receipts or other documents representing a cash withdrawal are not fraudulent. If the total of receipts plus cash is less than fifty dollars, then someone has probably taken money from the box without leaving a receipt.

Should these violations become serious, the best strategy is probably to eliminate the petty cash fund. However, one must bear in mind that this is a petty cash fund. So long as only a small balance is at stake, not much time or energy should be spent in controlling it. The time and energy would be much better spent in controlling the checking account and other important assets.

(8)   Prenumbered Documents

Even the smallest organization can take an important step toward internal control by using prenumbered documents. Whether they are checks, sales invoices, receipts or purchase orders, documents are a critical component of internal control. Prenumbering these documents ensures that genuine ones are not removed or fraudulent ones inserted. It is highly unlikely that an embezzler would go to the trouble of having a duplicate series of numbered documents printed even in a large organization, and certainly not in a small one. Prenumbered documents can help prevent fraud in cases like these:

- **Receipts**. Perhaps the most effective use of receipts is in the case of cash sales. Ordinarily, cash income is vulnerable to theft. But prenumbered receipts ensure that all cash is accounted for. Used receipts cannot be removed from the sequence to hide a cash shortage. The most common use occurs in restaurants where a waitress prepares the receipt, but does not handle cash—so there is no opportunity for fraud by her. The cashier accepts the cash, but cannot steal any because the numbered list of receipts shows the correct amount of sales. This technique also works for cash contributions which are collected in person (as opposed to through the mail) where receipts are given to donors as a matter of practice.

- **Checks**. The advantage of prenumbered checks is that blank checks cannot be stolen without a trace. Also, canceled checks for a fraudulent expense could not be replaced by canceled checks in the same amount for a legitimate expense.

A cash register acts much like prenumbered sales receipts. If all sales are rung up for the proper amount, cash cannot be stolen from the register without discovery. To help ensure that the correct amounts are rung up, the dollar display should be visible to customers and a register receipt should be given to them. Sometimes there is also a sign saying that customers will get their goods free if they do not get a receipt. The register total and the cash drawer should be checked at the end of each day.

(9)   The Annual Audit

Another way to combat fraud is to have an annual audit performed by a certified public accountant. Those who are not familiar with what an audit by a CPA entails should take note of these points:

- The audit does cost something (unless the association is fortunate enough to get a free audit which the CPA does for public relations purposes), and this cost should be compared to the possible fraud loss. Of course, audits have other advantages, such as finding errors, obtaining the confidence of members and bankers, and receiving accounting and business advice from the CPA.

- An audit is not designed to detect small frauds, and detection of even a large fraud cannot be guaranteed if there is collusion or a sophisticated plan of embezzlement. However, these are unlikely in a small organization. If there is some specific reason to suspect a fraud, then the CPA can extend his inquiry and generally get to the bottom of the matter.

- The mere knowledge of an audit will deter many would-be embezzlers, even though there is no guarantee that the audit will detect a fraud after it occurs. In fact, any work by a CPA, even if not an audit (for instance, a compilation or review), will have some deterrent effect. See Part II, I(5) for a description of the various levels of CPA report services.

(10)   Fidelity Bonds

To protect the association against large losses if controls are circumvented, the treasurer should consider purchasing a fidelity bond (sometimes called a "comprehensive dishonesty, disappearance and destruction policy"). Bonds can be purchased either on specific employees or on all employees in general (called blanket coverage). The amount of coverage should depend on the amount of financial exposure, and should be reviewed periodically. The premium cost may make bonds uneconomical for tiny organizations.

Sometimes it is not clear in the wording of a fidelity bond that association officers and directors, as well as employees, are covered. In this case, the insurance company or agency can be asked to acknowledge such coverage in a letter.

A bond should not be viewed as a substitute for controls, however. If there are no controls, bond premiums may be higher, and undetected losses may exceed the amount of bond coverage. In addition, if an association is to collect under a bond, it must first detect the fraud. To detect it, the association needs some kind of controls. Furthermore, bonding companies will not pay for losses caused by honest errors or for losses arising from reliance on misleading financial information. Controls are needed to help avoid these losses.

Besides compensating an organization for fraud losses, bonding companies provide additional advantages. They investigate the background of bonded employees, and if there is a fraud, are more likely to prosecute the embezzler than the employer association. Sophisticated embezzlers are usually aware of this, which acts as a deterrent.

(11) Safeguarding Cash in a Public Place

The treasurer should be responsible for arranging to safeguard large amounts of cash that the association may collect in a public place where it is visible to strangers and vulnerable to theft. This situation occurs when many people pay cash at the door on attending an association social function or a performance.

The person handling cash and tickets as a crowd enters a hall should not be expected to do the job alone because making change, dispensing tickets, and possibly checking an attendance list and distributing name tags all divert one's attention from the cash box. A second person, whether a member volunteer or an office staff person, should be present to assist so that one of the two can concentrate on handling the cash.

When cash collections have reached a large amount, the treasurer should arrange to remove some of the cash from the collection point, giving the cash handler a signed receipt for it. The treasurer can carry the money on his person, or may be able to turn it over to the hotel or restaurant management for safekeeping. The important point is to move large amounts of cash away from a vulnerable place near an outside entrance where people are congregating.

Associations that hold regularly scheduled fund-raising events, such as Bingo nights, should take special measures to secure their cash when removing it from the premises after the event, and especially at night.

(12) Prompt Depositing of Checks Received

To the extent practical, the treasurer should promptly deposit checks received into the association's bank account. Loose checks have an uncanny knack of disappearing into piles of papers, which leads to frustrating and time-consuming searches. There are also the risks that the checks may be stolen, or that a check writer's account will sometime later be closed or overdrawn. If the checks are received for the sale of merchandise, the association might inadvertently continue to make sales to someone writing bad checks, because bad checks are usually detected only by depositing them.

Another important reason for prompt depositing is to avoid annoying the check writer. If checks are held beyond the end of the month, the check writer will discover that the check is still uncashed when the check writer's own bank statement is reconciled. This person may then conclude that the association does not need or appreciate receiving the money, particularly in the case of donations. The treasurer will also receive phone calls from worried check writers asking if their checks were actually received, and the time spent fielding these calls may be more than the time needed for a deposit in the first place.

Of course, in a very small association it may be impractical for the treasurer to always make deposits immediately. However, at the very least a special effort should be made several days before month-end to deposit any remaining checks on hand to avoid the problem discussed above of check writers discovering that their checks are uncashed.

(C)   Monitoring Financial Trends

(1)   Reimbursement of Expenses

The treasurer should take the initiative in setting an association policy on the reimbursement of out-of-pocket expenses incurred by officers and members and monitor adherence to the policy. The rules should be put in writing and distributed to everyone affected by them. An association that does not have such a policy can be steadily drained of funds, and questionable reimbursements paid to some individuals can cause dissension among the membership.

A reimbursement policy statement might cover these points:

- A list of association officers and representatives who are normally entitled to reimbursement of expenses;
- A list of items, such as postage and long-distance telephone calls, that are normally reimbursable;
- A list of items that are not normally reimbursable, such as meals, drinks, taxi fares or entertainment;
- Rules for travel expenses, including use of a private car;
- A ceiling figure for reimbursement without prior authorization;
- A procedure for prior authorization of an extraordinary expense.

When dealing with a guest speaker or other non-member, the association should explain at the outset, in writing, its policy and expense limit.

The treasurer should insist that every request for reimbursement be submitted in proper form. The request should be typewritten, or in ink, with date and signature, stating how the money was spent and for what association purpose. The treasurer may have to explain that informal and cryptic notes, using first names only or nicknames without clear purpose or date, are not sufficient, and that they can invite the suspicion of an auditor or an Internal Revenue Service examiner.

(2)   Controlling Free Admissions and Giveaways

The treasurer should try to limit an association's practice of granting gratis admissions to luncheons and dinners, free drinks at social hours, and giveaways of association property such as publications—all under the heading of hospitality or public relations. An overly-generous practice in this area can lead to sizeable financial loss to the association.

Giveaways are often made by several different people who may not realize the extent to which others are doing the same. The head of the speakers committee may permit a luncheon speaker to bring along two family members, all being guests for whom the treasury must pay. A hospitality chairman may authorize more complimentary drinks from the bar than courtesy really requires. Or the publications committee may distribute an undue number of free copies of a book that the association has published as a fund-raising device. Each of these officers may consider his or her own giveaway as petty, without realizing that together they add up to a considerable total.

To avoid misunderstanding and embarrassment, the association should set limits to all giveaways as a matter of policy. Then the treasurer should remind others, when necessary, of the need to adhere firmly to the policy.

(3)   Fellowship Expenses

The treasurer should take responsibility for establishing a policy governing fellowship expenses in case of the illness or death of an association member, such as the cost of flowers, remembrance donations to a medical fund or church, and the like. At a time of emotional stress, it can be embarrassing to the treasurer to act as guardian of the association's money, and thus appear to be indifferent to the feelings of others. It is therefore useful to the treasurer for the association to have an established policy governing fellowship expenditures which all are expected to observe.

An association can establish the policy that all fellowship expenses are to be borne by those individuals who wish to contribute, and that no money from the association treasury is to be used. This policy can protect the officers from possible criticism that they are spending the association's money on their own friends, whereas they would not use treasury funds in case of the illness or death of a member they did not know, or one in a distant city.

Another policy might be to establish a spending limit in case of a member's illness or death, leaving the choice of the exact form of gift or remembrance to the president or to a fellowship committee. Or there might be a more detailed system of spending limits, with one maximum for current officers and past presidents, another for the rest of the membership.

If association funds are used for fellowship expenses, the treasurer can report on the total at the end of the fiscal year when emotions have cooled, along with any recommendations he may have as to their combined impact on the association treasury. In this way, the spending policy can be evaluated without reference to any individual case.

(4)   Controlling the Office Work Load

One way in which an organization's operating costs escalate almost without anyone noticing is through a step-by-step increase in the work load placed on the salaried office staff. Although increased office work by itself does not always lead to higher expenditures, it can often lead to these results:

- The need at times to ask the staff to work overtime, for pay;
- Hiring temporary workers to help out at certain times or for certain activities;
- Increased auxiliary costs required by a new project, such as stationery and postage used in an additional mailing, or a rental typewriter needed by a temporary helper;
- Finally, when it reaches a certain point, an increased office work load leads to pressure on the association to add additional paid positions.

In order to control an association's headquarters costs, therefore, the treasurer should pay close attention to the tendency of other officers and committee heads to drop more and more work on the office staff, rather than carry it out themselves.

(5)   Employee Salaries and Benefits

Since the cost of the salaried office staff is a major expense for many organizations, the treasurer should be consulted when starting salaries are determined and when increases are given. He should also be among those who determine the package of nonsalary benefits covering each employee, which may include:

- Hospitalization or other health funds paid for by the employer;
- A year-end or annual bonus;
- The holiday schedule, which should be fixed and made clear to all employees (particularly with respect to the policy if a holiday falls on a weekend);

- Vacations and sick leave. A written policy should specify whether unused vacation and sick leave can be carried over from year-to-year, and whether they will be "cashed out" at the end of employment. It should also specify if vacation is earned a little bit each month, or all at once at year-end.

- Contributions to a pension fund.

By keeping track of these various benefits, the treasurer can help the governing board obtain a realistic picture of the full cost of each employee and of what benefits the association can afford.

With respect to pension, insurance, and similar matters, an attorney or CPA should be consulted if all employees are not given equal coverage, because of ever-changing IRS nondiscrimination requirements.

(6) Expected Income

The treasurer should keep a checklist of sources and dates of expected association income and see to the prompt collection of monies owed. These could include such items as rent from a tenant, royalties due from a publisher for a book prepared by the association, or delinquent dues promised by a certain date.

(D) Investing Idle Cash

Proper investing of excess cash balances may not be significant to some small organizations but can be critical for others. There are two things to be considered: First, assets must be safeguarded from loss; and second, the maximum possible income should be earned on idle cash balances. Sometimes, but not always, these goals may be inconsistent. The right kind of investment policy will vary somewhat from one kind of organization to another, so the concepts that follow are only principles, not hard and fast rules.

Receipts should be deposited promptly, usually by the next day. Undeposited receipts may be lost or stolen. In addition, these idle funds, plus excess amounts in the checking account, could be earning interest.

Generally, no more should be left in the checking account than is necessary for expenses over a reasonable period, allowing a margin of safety for unexpected payments. The length of the time period is relative to the amounts involved. In a small organization where no more than a few hundred dollars are in the account, a period of perhaps a month or more may be used since investment of the excess funds would not produce much income. But in a large organization where hundreds of thousands of dollars are at stake, the checking account should have no more than a single day's needs. For instance,

$100,000.00 which would not be needed until the next day can generate a significant amount of income overnight, and over the course of a year such an organization might earn several thousand dollars through overnight investment of this excess. Moving excess funds out of the checking account also helps prevent someone from crippling the organization by writing a huge fraudulent check and then disappearing.

An exception to the above rule may occur if a checking account that earns interest is available. The treasurer should inquire at a bank about eligibility requirements and restrictions for such accounts. Since excess funds do earn interest in such an account, the need to reinvest is less critical. However, other investment opportunities may be available that yield a considerably higher rate. Thus, significant excess funds should not be left even in an interest-bearing checking account if a safe but higher rate is available elsewhere.

Common investments for excess funds include money market funds, certificates of deposit, or U.S. Government securities. These provide the maximum yield which is consistent with reasonable safety. However, each type of investment differs somewhat from the others. Money market funds (or savings accounts) may require a minimum balance (usually $500.00 or more), but provide the best liquidity. Deposits and withdrawals usually can be made at any time in any amount. Interest is paid at a variable rate. Such funds, though, are often not insured (unless issued by a bank or a savings and loan), meaning that if a fund goes bankrupt, the organization will lose some or all of its money. Certificates of deposit also require a minimum balance, but offer a guaranteed rate of interest over the term of the certificate (three months to four years). Liquidity is much poorer since there is a substantial penalty for withdrawal before the term of the certificate is completed. Certificates are insured by the federal government, but only up to the first $100,000.00 of deposits which the organization has in this particular bank. Deposits in excess of $100,000.00 are not insured and may be lost if the bank becomes insolvent. If the organization has more than $100,000.00 in deposits, an easy solution is to spread the deposits over several banks so that no more than $100,000.00 is left with any one. U.S. Government securities (primarily treasury bills) also require a minimum purchase price ($1,000.00), and the yield is fixed over the life of the security. Unlike certificates of deposit, government securities are liquid since they can be sold at any time. Payment of principal and interest on securities issued by the U.S. Treasury and certain federal agencies is guaranteed if held to maturity—but if sold before maturity, there could be an increase or decrease in value depending on market interest rates.

There are, of course, many other forms of investments: stocks, bonds, commodities, real estate and so forth. They offer the possibility of higher returns but also involve the risk of loss. Real estate also lacks liquidity. The organization may decide on one of these investments in the hope of higher earnings. However, this decision should be made by the organization's governing body or by an investment advisory committee, and not by the treasurer acting alone.

(E) Custody of Books and Records

The treasurer is responsible for the safe custody of financial records. On taking office he should check to see that the records of past years are on hand, that they are kept in a safe place, that they are clearly marked, and that the office staff knows where they are. This makes it easier to find the necessary entries in order to answer inquiries from the governing board, the association's accountant, an Internal Revenue Service auditor, a vendor or an association member.

The day-to-day custody of the current-year financial records is the responsibility of the office staff, acting under direction of the treasurer. In a small organization that has neither office nor paid staff, the treasurer should take responsibility for safeguarding the current records either in his home or at his office. He should avoid carrying the records frequently between home, work place and the association meeting place because the danger of loss is thus increased.

When the records are kept in the association office, the treasurer and others needing to work with them elsewhere should use duplicate copies whenever possible. If an original document must be removed from the office, however, the borrower should record the removal, with date, in a sign-out book kept in the office for that purpose.

(1) Treasury Filing System

The treasury files should be organized alphabetically by subject and labeled so the contents are easy to find. Labeling should be clear to all—including the office staff and a successor treasurer. There is no excuse for "keeping the file in my head," and the treasurer who tries to do this is unfair to others in the association. He may think he can remember all aspects of his job during his term— but his successor may know nothing about them unless they are clearly recorded and the outgoing treasurer briefs him on his new duties and the procedures of the position.

Files in cabinets and record books should be labeled with key words that are meaningful to all concerned. The label TAXES, Federal: Form 941, for instance, is much clearer than simply Form 941. Most people do not even know what Form 941 is or what it has to do with an association treasury. In labeling treasury files, it is best to use broad categories as first headings, then follow with subheadings—rather than use minor subjects as a primary entry. Of course, when it appears that a change in file headings would be useful, the treasurer should make the change.

There should be an alphabetical list or guide to the main subjects in the treasury files, kept where the treasurer and others can use it. A handy place is in the front of the first file drawer by the first "A" entry. Brief notes added to the headings on the guide can help others find which folder contains a certain item.

Guide to Treasurer's Files, Alphabetical

Accountant's Report (annual financial statements, past three years)

Bank (checking acct. at _____ Bank, statements, checkbook, etc.)

Bequests (incl. Codicil form)

Bills Paid (chronological; latest in front)

Contributions (incl. form acknowledgment letter)

Correspondence (not classified elsewhere)

Dues Collection

Employee Benefits (holidays, vacation, hospitalization, etc.)

Employee Payroll Records

Employee Payroll Taxes (incl. reports to IRS and State)

Investment Funds (money market acct. at _____ Fund)

IRS (tax returns, correspondence, chronological)

The treasurer should file papers in the appropriate folders promptly, or have someone else do it regularly. He should avoid having an accumulation of unfiled material in which another person may not be able to find a needed item.

(2)   Action Guides to the Files

The treasurer should write a brief, clear action guide or memorandum sheet for each treasury function, giving its purpose and the essential information needed to carry it out. Each guide should be placed where it can be seen easily—preferably attached to the inside front cover of the file folder devoted to the given subject. The action guide helps the treasurer, the office staff and the successor treasurer find quickly what they need to know for that activity without having to search through many papers in the folder to locate a detail.

The action guide to a file labeled BANK ACCOUNT, for instance, might include the account number, name and mailing address of the bank, name and telephone number of the bank officer responsible for the association account, rate of interest paid on the association savings account, procedure for ordering new checks, minimum balance required to avoid penalty, and anything else useful.

The action guides to file folders on payment of Social Security, wage withholding, and unemployment taxes and the like may be more detailed. They should include the current tax being paid and how it is calculated, the association's taxpayer number issued by the IRS, frequency and due date of filing reports, name and number of the form used in reporting, location of the forms in the office, source of a fresh supply of forms, and warnings of errors to avoid.

These action guides in the treasury files can be most useful when the outgoing treasurer instructs his successor on his responsibilities. If the action guides are kept up to date and are in the proper place, the liaison procedure becomes much easier. The action guides also make it less likely that the association will be injured by errors of omission caused by someone's forgetfulness or absence. And they can save the day if the association should lose its treasurer suddenly without his having made a proper liaison with his successor.

(3)   Cleaning the Files and Document Retention

At least once during his term the treasurer should clean the files so that useless old records do not obscure needed material that is current or recent. A simple first step is to remove folders from the previous year, each labeled by subject and date, and put them in a storage space where they can be retrieved if needed. This would help the treasurer keep the records on the current year's annual banquet, for instance, separate from the records of the previous year's banquet. Yet the earlier ones would be available if they are needed for cost comparison.

The next issue is how long records for prior years must be kept in storage before they can be thrown away. Although this seems like a simple question,

the exact answer depends on the particular document and the particular association. For simplicity, documents can be divided into three groups:

- <u>Short-term documents</u>. These are "source" documents of a financial
  nature—such as bank statements, checkbooks, canceled checks,
  deposit tickets, receipts, bills, payroll tax returns (Federal Forms 940
  and 941, and state unemployment tax forms), employee earnings
  records and donations lists—which should be kept for a minimum of
  four years. After then, it is probably safe to dispose of them if the
  treasurer checks first with an attorney or certified public accountant
  to make sure they will not be needed.

- <u>Longer-term records</u>. These are the cash receipts and cash expenditure books which should be kept for at least ten years and preferably
  indefinitely. Since check numbers are preserved here, if a copy of a
  check is needed after the canceled checks are thrown away, one can
  be obtained from the bank.

- <u>Permanent records</u>. These should be kept as long as the association is
  in existence and for at least several years afterward (see an attorney
  for exactly how long). Examples are the articles of incorporation,
  bylaws, minutes, application and approval forms related to tax-
  exempt status, annual income tax returns (usually Federal Form 990,
  including any proof of mailing), annual financial statements, stock
  certificates, deeds, and long-term leases, mortgages or agreements.
  Of course, the association should also retain anything which,
  although not needed for legal purposes, might be of historical value
  in a future anniversary article or yearbook such as newsletters, membership lists, photographs or special correspondence.

If in doubt whether a document can be disposed of, keep it—or at least get
advice from an attorney or certified public accountant before throwing it away.

When disposing of old documents it is not necessary to shred or burn them
unless there are confidential records or other special circumstances.

Chapter 6. BUSINESS DEALINGS WITH OUTSIDERS

(A) Vendors: Reviewing and Paying Bills
    (1) Pay Bills with Eyes Open
    (2) Monitor Continuing, Repeated Expenses
    (3) Keep Original Bills

(B) Banks, Investment Funds

(C) Landlord and Tenants

(D) Secretary of State

(E) Federal and State Tax Agencies

(F) Insurance Companies or Agency

(G) Soliciting Funds

(H) Public Inspection of Tax Documents

CHAPTER 6

Business Dealings with Outsiders

(A)   Vendors: Reviewing and Paying Bills

(1)   Pay Bills with Eyes Open

In dealings with printers, stationery suppliers and other vendors, the treasurer should always examine bills submitted to him for payment. He should not assume that every bill reaching him should be paid as written. He should be alert to situations such as:

- The excessive bill—which might have been an honest mistake or might have been intentionally padded by a vendor to test whether the association is careful in spending its money;

- A second bill for the same service or merchandise prepared and mailed by a vendor shortly before receiving the association's check in payment for the earlier bill;

- The premature bill—for merchandise not yet delivered or service not yet performed;

- A misdirected bill—one sent to the association incorrectly through confusion in the vendor's office with the name of another organization.

The treasurer can save time in checking the validity of bills for payment if he arranges a system of bill validation by others who know what certain bills are for. When he receives bills for transactions that he was not directly involved with, the treasurer should insist that one competent person—an officer, committee head or staff member—initial and date the bills of which they have direct knowledge. Initialing should be understood as that person's approval of the bill for payment.

Carrolton Stationers			
1420 Smith Lane			
Carrolton, Illinois 62803			August 24, 20XX
(555) 812-4600			(Net due 30 days)

STATEMENT

Quantity	Item	Unit Price	Total
2 Boxes	#10 Envelopes	$ 8.45	$16.90
1 Ream	Parchment Ecru letterhead	22.44	22.44
	Tax:		$ 3.93
	TOTAL:		$43.27

OK to pay.
A.B. 9/12/XX

Pd. 9/15/xx
G.R. #3145

> Approval by person
> responsible

> Treasurer's record of
> payment date and
> check number

Certain regular bills, such as monthly rent bills, can be paid by the treasurer on his own initiative because he is familiar with them. But it is still his duty to examine them for accuracy before making payment.

(2)   Monitor Continuing, Repeated Expenses

The treasurer has special responsibility to monitor the prices charged the association for continuing, repeated items such as hotel and restaurant charges for luncheon and dinner meetings, or the landlord's charges for building operating expenses included in the rent bills, or a printer's bills for producing and mailing a periodical. If the treasurer observes creeping inflation in these charges, he should examine the increases to see if they are justified. Where it is necessary, he should notify the governing body with recommendations for action to prevent a serious long-term loss.

The treasurer should be alert to the "low-ball" technique by which some suppliers attract a customer by offering a low price at the start, then gradually increase their charges on subsequent bills, hoping that the customer does not notice the increase. To guard against this, an association can propose a contract for a year or more with a clear understanding of the price to be paid. Most reputable suppliers welcome such a contract, which offers security to both parties.

(3)   Keep Original Bills

When paying bills, the treasurer should keep the original bill (or "top copy") for the association files and return the carbon copy or duplicate to the vendor if it is requested. The association, as the customer being billed, has a right to the original clear bill for its records. If any part of the bill is indistinct, or if it requires correction, the corrections should be made clearly in ink before the bill is paid and filed.

When a check is drawn to pay a bill, the bill should be plainly marked "Paid" with the date of payment or the check number before it is filed. In case of later need, the record of payment can be readily traced to the check stub from either the payment date or the check number. If further proof of payment is required, the canceled check can then be located with the monthly bank statements and a copy sent to the vendor to settle the issue.

(B)   Banks, Investment Funds

The treasurer is usually the association officer responsible for dealing with the bank where it has a checking account, and with investment institutions holding the association's interest-bearing accounts. On taking office, the new treasurer should make certain that all these financial institutions recognize his credentials. The procedures for establishing credentials, in cooperation with the outgoing treasurer, are explained in Chapter 3(A)(2).

Once the authority of the incoming treasurer to represent the association with financial institutions is established, he should become acquainted with a bank officer to make that person familiar with the treasurer's name, signature, face and telephone voice. This can save the treasurer considerable time and trouble in later dealings because the bank officer will know the association account and its methods of operation.

If things run smoothly, there may be little occasion to call the bank or to visit it except to make deposits into the association account. However, the treasurer or an office staff member acting for him should not hesitate to call on the bank to explain a service charge on a monthly statement or to explain any bank procedure that is not clearly spelled out in a bank mailing. Too often customers feel over-awed by a financial organization and hesitate to ask for that which is their right—a clear explanation in lay terms of every transaction reported on a statement. The bank statement is supposed to be a communication from the bank to the depositor/customer. Therefore it should be put in language and symbols that the customer understands.

Should the treasurer run into difficulty in reconciling the bank statement (Chapter 4(G)), he may get assistance from the bank officer he deals with. As said earlier, the chances are overwhelming that the bank is correct in its figures. But if there is an irreconcilable difference between the bank statement and the treasurer's calculations, the matter should be called to the bank's attention. When this is done, an efficient bank officer can often help find the discrepancy between the two sets of figures.

Dealings with investment funds are usually far less frequent for the association treasurer than contacts with the checking account bank. The principles are the same: establish the incoming treasurer's credentials through the fund's signature validation procedures; examine each statement and reconcile it with the known transactions (deposits and withdrawals) and interest earned; and attempt to get the name and telephone number of one fund officer who is familiar with the association account.

It is up to the treasurer to read the various mailings that banks and investment funds send to customers so he can keep up with new services the bank may offer, as well as with changes in interest rates, special charges or reporting periods. If there are changes that an incoming treasurer might not know, the outgoing treasurer should inform his successor of them.

(C)   Landlord and Tenants

When an association rents office space, the treasurer should see that both the chosen location and the length of lease are carefully considered. A long-term lease should be avoided if there is a chance that the association might want to move its office elsewhere while the lease is still in force, or might require less space, or find the building and the neighborhood deteriorating.

If the association should sublet part of its space to a tenant, it should avoid doing so on a long-term basis because the tenant may be difficult to displace when the association later requires the space for itself.

Unless the association has established a relationship of trust over a period of time with the landlord or with a tenant, it is wise to submit a draft lease to an attorney with experience in such contracts. The cost of an attorney's review is generally modest, and a trained eye may find points that should be changed for the association's protection. Such a review should certainly be made if the treasurer and other officers are dealing with the landlord for the first time and have little or no experience in renting office space.

Where the proposed lease is long-term, an attorney's review may be needed even if there is a good relationship with the current landlord. This is because the landlord may sell the building during the term of the lease, and the new landlord may not be as easy to get along with. Without an attorney's review, the new landlord could take advantage of the often unread "fine print" in the lease to the association's detriment.

The treasurer and other officers should also be sure that when they do sign a lease that only the association itself is liable for payment of rent—not themselves personally. For this reason, watch out for the words "guarantee" or "surety" in the lease, and when signing, write, "Treasurer" after your name (or "President," "Trustee," *etc.*) to show that you are merely acting as a representative of the association, not as an individual tenant.

(D)   Secretary of State

One of the greatest sources of difficulty in managing a new and growing organization is dealing with state (and federal) government agencies. This happens because there is often no automatic notification system by which an association is told that it should register with the state, usually with the Secretary of State, and send annual reports to the proper state agencies. In some associations the registration responsibility falls to the secretary. An organization with an alert attorney or other person experienced in these matters among its leadership will inform the governing board about this. Frequently, however, an organization finds out well after the fact that it has been delinquent under state law in failing to register or file annual reports for the past several years.

The treasurer, as business manager of the association, should be mindful of the need to observe the state law governing organizations, both those for profit and not for profit. Upon taking office, a conscientious treasurer should inquire into the legal status of the organization and, if necessary, should see that it is properly registered and that annual reports are filed with the Secretary of State. If there is doubt, he can write or call the Secretary of State to obtain a copy of whatever statute and printed matter is available on the laws governing associations that operate within the state. If necessary, he should insist that the association retain a competent attorney to guide it through the registration procedures and the filing of any reports required, including financial reports.

State governments are usually less concerned with a small local club that neither solicits contributions from the public nor has any employees. But when a new organization reaches the point where it solicits money from non-members or hires employees, the state is concerned—because the laws governing fraudulent soliciting are involved in the one case, and various social insurance laws protecting workers are involved in the other.

State laws governing associations vary so widely in the United States that it is not practical to discuss here the details of registering and reporting in fifty jurisdictions. Part II, A & B of this book offers an explanation of the generally accepted procedures for incorporating an association and fulfilling state requirements, to which readers concerned with this matter should turn.

(E)   Federal and State Tax Agencies

The treasurer is the association officer who should take responsibility for filing the required reports and, where necessary, make tax payments to both federal and state tax agencies. If he does not see that the reports are filed and the taxes paid, no one else is likely to do so. It is therefore most important that he be aware of what the federal and state laws require, and that he see that the requirements are met on time. Substantial penalties are imposed for neglect that the association can ill afford to pay. Nor is there any reason why these duties should be neglected once the treasurer knows what is expected of him.

Unless a new treasurer steps into a situation where his predecessor can give him all the information he needs, he should seek the guidance of a specialist experienced in the legal and tax regulations governing associations. In most metropolitan areas he should find an attorney or a certified public accountant who has specialized in advising nonprofit associations. The treasurer can ask for a recommendation from the executive of another association, or he can inquire through the local chapter of the state bar association or the state society of CPAs. Once the treasurer and his mentor have established a schedule of filings and tax payments to be made through the year and the treasurer understands the forms and how to complete them, he and the office staff can usually carry out the work easily enough. But it is often necessary that a professionally trained specialist be consulted at the start so that the legal requirements are met. Making this initial contact with a specialist also facilitates obtaining information should the treasurer have questions later on.

As said above in regard to state registration laws, the state tax laws governing associations also differ widely. They should be discussed with a specialist practicing in the state concerned.

Federal law concerns the association in two ways: First, as an entity that may or may not be exempt from income taxation; and second, as an employer responsible for withheld wage taxes and FICA (Social Security) taxes. These taxes must first be collected, then paid; and they must be accounted for in periodic reports to the Internal Revenue Service.

As an entity, a tax-exempt association may have to file IRS Form 990 annually. From this report the IRS determines whether the association is continuing to operate for the same purposes that it declared when it obtained tax-exempt status. Form 990 must be filed with the IRS by the 15th day of the fifth month following the end of its fiscal year. This means, for example, that an association with a June 30 year-end must file by November 15. Failure to file on time can lead to a daily penalty starting on the date on which the filing was due. If there is good reason, an association can ask ahead of time for an extension of the due date, but it is good practice to file on time to avoid difficulties. For further information on filing Form 990, see Part II, B(1)(d).

As an employer, the association must make periodic deposits of taxes withheld from its employees (adding the employer's matching share of FICA tax) to its bank, which then forwards the money to the IRS. The record of earnings and deductions (*see* Chapter 8) details the amounts that the association has withheld from each employee's pay for federal and state taxes, and is the starting point in determining the amount owed to the taxing agencies. The IRS provides the association with a supply of Form 8109 coupons to fill out and accompany each deposit of withheld taxes to the bank.

The method of calculating the amount of taxes to be withheld from employee paychecks and the government requirements for reporting their wages on Form W-2 are covered in Chapter 8.

The rules for determining the exact due date for depositing federal taxes with the bank are complicated and are discussed in detail in Part II, C. However, if you wish to avoid confusion and the risk of penalties, you can comply with the deadlines by following these two simple guidelines:

- If you are sure that the association's total federal income tax withheld plus the employees' and employer's shares of FICA tax will be less than $2,500.00 for the entire quarter, you do not need to make advance deposits. You can simply send a check to the IRS together with Form 941 before the last day of the month following the calendar quarter (*see* below). Usually an association will have less than $2,500.00 in tax for the quarter only if its payroll is limited to one or two employees.

- Otherwise simply deposit all the federal taxes owed (income tax withholding plus both shares of FICA tax) every payday, or no later than three business days afterwards. Following this rule may result in the association paying taxes a little sooner than required, but will generally avoid penalties.

The treasurer should keep a current record, with which the office staff head (if any) should be familiar, of federal and state taxes as they are paid. Receipts from the bank confirm that the federal tax deposits were safely received. Unless taxes are deposited every payday, there is an interval between paying the staff and paying the withheld taxes, and the treasurer can easily forget to deposit the taxes on time. (Remember: The government sends no advance reminders about the due date.) And since there has been a trend toward increased penalties for failure to pay taxes of all kinds on time, the treasurer might establish a reminder system under which another officer or employee consults the tax payment record and, if necessary, advises him that a deposit is due.

The treasurer should also be aware that if the association does not pay its withheld payroll taxes, certain directors and officers of the association (including the treasurer) may be personally liable to the IRS for those taxes—in other words, the treasurer may wind up paying those taxes out of his own pocket if the association does not do so. This warning is especially applicable to treasurers of associations with cash flow problems where the association is often tempted to put payment of taxes on the back burner.

As mentioned above, the IRS requires the association/employer to file Form 941 ("Employer's Quarterly Federal Tax Return") every calendar quarter by the last day of the month following the end of the quarter. For example, Form 941 for the first quarter, which ends March 31st, would be due on or before April 30th. Form 941 is sent directly to the IRS and consists of a summary of taxes withheld from employees and deposited during the preceding quarter. Of course, Form 941 should be filled out carefully so that the association does not overstate or understate the taxes owed or deposits made. Otherwise there will be penalties. If a deposit was somehow overlooked, it should be made at once before Form 941 is filled out for the quarter just elapsed.

The organization (unless it is a section 501(c)(3) organization) must also file Form 940 with the IRS each January 31st to report and pay federal unemployment (FUTA) taxes. These are discussed further in Part II, C.

If, without withholding any taxes, the association has paid $600.00 or more during the calendar year to a casual or part-time worker who is not considered an employee, or to an outside contractor or business that is not a corporation, or to a lawyer (whether incorporated or not), it must report this to the IRS annually. Form 1099-MISC ("Miscellaneous Compensation") is used for this, one copy going to the IRS and the other to the person who was paid. Form 1099-MISC must be given to the worker by January 31st of the following year, and the filing with the IRS must occur by February 28th. To comply with this requirement, the treasurer should keep a record of all money paid to non-employees during the year, together with the Social Security number of each such person, preferably by having the person fill out IRS Form W-9. Failure to have the Social Security number or to make a correct filing can lead to substantial penalties.

With respect to the distinction between an employee and a non-employee for these purposes, there is no clear dividing line. Generally a person working within the association office on a regular schedule is considered an employee, even if part time. Persons who set their own schedules and provide their own work areas, or hold themselves out to the public as independent businesses, often are non-employees. An attorney or CPA should be consulted if substantial payments are made to a person whose status as an employee or non-employee is unclear. For further information, see Chapter 8(M).

(F) Insurance Companies or Agency

At least yearly the treasurer should see that there is a review of the association's insurance program in order to make certain that the organization, its officers and employees are protected with suitable insurance at reasonable cost. Beyond that he should see that the association establishes guidelines for its insurance program, and that it designates who has the authority to increase or change coverage when necessary. A small association may require no insurance except perhaps a fidelity bond covering those who handle funds. A large association, however, may require insurance coverage in its several roles, such as landlord, tenant, operator of a dining room, supplier of services, employer, and perhaps others. The exposure to risk varies widely and can change from one year to another. An association therefore may wish to appoint a standing committee on insurance to review the program at regular intervals.

The following types of insurance are commonly used by associations:

- Fidelity Bond (also known as a Comprehensive Dishonesty, Disappearance and Destruction Policy)—to protect the association against loss from theft by officers or employees;

- Comprehensive General Liability Policy—to protect the association against a wide variety of claims such as accidental injury on its premises to a member, guest or employee. Be sure that the association's officers, directors, employees, members and volunteers are also covered by this policy;

- Worker's Compensation and Employer's Liability Policy—usually required by state law to protect the association against claims arising from an employee's injury at work, and to compensate the employee for such injury;

- <u>Disability</u>—to provide income during the recovery period for a disabled employee;

- <u>Life, Hospitalization and Major Medical Insurance</u>—for employees.

The task of keeping current with policy renewals can be handled easily when the association deals with one reliable insurance agency. The agency can send bills on designated dates, and can advise the association on the most suitable coverage for the price. The treasurer or the insurance committee should consider such advice with care and avoid being over-sold on insurance that is not really needed.

(G)   Soliciting Funds

If your association solicits donations, it may be necessary to obtain a permit (state or city), and there may also be an annual reporting requirement. The offices of the Secretary of State and the city clerk should be contacted for details.

If payments to your organization are <u>not</u> tax deductible as charitable contributions (*see* Part II, R(1)), and the association has over $100,000.00 of annual gross receipts, Part II, R(1) also discusses the notice of non-deductibility statement which is required by the IRS to accompany any solicitation of funds.

Conversely, if contributions to the organization <u>are</u> tax deductible, and if solicitations are made and the donor is given something significant in return for a contribution (such as a dinner or a magazine subscription), the prospective donor must be given a written statement (usually printed in the solicitation materials) informing the person of the value of the item to be received in return, and that the person's tax-deductible contribution must be reduced by this amount.

Also, if contributions are tax deductible, anyone donating $250.00 or more at one time must be given a letter or statement from your organization verifying the date and amount of the contribution (for non-cash contributions, give a description, but specifying a value is not required). The document must also state whether the donor received anything in return and, if so, what it was and its estimated value. The letter or statement can be sent to the donor right after the contribution is made, or a cumulative statement for the year can be sent to the donor before the donor's own tax return is filed. An example of such a letter is shown here:

(The Organization Letterhead)

September 28, XXXX

Mr. John Q. Doe
1000 First Street
Anytown, IA 50010

Dear Mr. Doe:

This letter is to acknowledge and thank you for your contribution of $300.00 on September 15, XXXX.

[or]

This letter is to acknowledge and thank you for your contribution of 100 shares of Acme, Inc. Common stock on September 15, XXXX.

[and]

You did not receive any goods or services from our organization in return for this contribution.

[or]

You received a dinner for two valued in total at $50.00 in exchange for this contribution. For tax purposes, you must reduce your contributions deduction by this $50.00.

Very truly yours,

Organization Treasurer

The organization does not have to send this letter or statement to the IRS. The letter or statement is also not required where a donor makes only donations which are smaller than $250.00 each, even though the cumulative total for the year is more than $250.00. For instance, someone donating $10.00 a week to a church for fifty weeks need not be given a letter or statement even though the annual total is $500.00.

Of course, there is never any harm in providing a letter or statement even when not required, and this may enhance the organization's goodwill with donors.

(H)   Public Inspection of Tax Documents

A tax-exempt organization must comply with some possibly burdensome rules regarding public inspection of certain tax documents. These consist of the three most recent tax returns, if any were required to be filed (generally Form 990), the application for exempt status (Form 1023 or 1024), and the IRS letter approving exempt status. The names and addresses of donors may be withheld or blocked out unless the organization is a private foundation (Part II, Q). Form 990-T concerning unrelated business income, if any (Part II, O), may also be withheld.

If the organization does not have a regular office, a reasonable time and place must be made available upon request for this inspection. Otherwise, the documents must be available for inspection at the organization's office during normal business hours. Anyone, for any reason (or no reason at all) may request an inspection; the inspection right is not limited to members, donors, or someone demonstrating a "justifiable" need. The person may also request copies to keep, and these must be made for the person unless the documents are already posted on the Internet. (Internet posting can be either on the organization's own web site, or on a nationwide "archive" of charitable tax returns such as www.guidestar.org.) If paper copies are made for the person, the organization may make a reasonable charge for copying (and mailing, if applicable). To be safe, any such charge should be comparable to the charges of nearby photocopy shops. In lieu of "hosting" a possibly time-consuming, in-person inspection, the person may simply be provided with copies and sent away; however, no charge can be made for these copies unless the individual is also offered the in-person inspection option. Note that Internet posting, by itself, does not eliminate the need to offer the in-person inspection option. It only eliminates the need to make copies for the person.

If the individual shows up in person, the documents must be made available immediately (or if this causes an unusual hardship, no more than five days later). If the request is made by mail, the organization has 30 days to fulfill the request.

A small organization not involved in any publicity or controversy may never receive a document request. But if there is dissension within the organization, or the organization is in the news or is associated with a controversial cause, then there is a "high risk" that a document request will likely come from someone such as a disgruntled member, news reporter, prospective donor or political agitator.

There are substantial monetary penalties for failure to comply with any of these inspection requirements, so the treasurer would be well-advised (especially for "high risk" organizations mentioned above) to create a special "public inspection" file containing an extra copy of all the required documents in one place with the donors' names already blocked out in advance. The organization's only copies should not be used for this purpose because of the possible deletion of donors' names and the risk of papers "walking off" at the end of the inspection.

The file can be quickly whipped out when someone requests an inspection, and anyone filling in during the treasurer's absence from the office should be familiar with where the file is and the procedures pertaining to inspection (the procedures might be written on the cover of the file, or a photocopy of these pages might simply be included).

Note that if the organization is not tax-exempt, these disclosure rules do not apply. Also, churches, while tax-exempt, generally do not prepare any of the pertinent documents, and thus there is usually nothing for them to disclose.

Chapter 7. RELATIONS WITH THE MEMBERSHIP

(A)   Membership Dues
    (1)   Who Sets the Dues?
    (2)   Flat or Variable Dues
    (3)   Frequency of Dues Payment
    (4)   Dues Refunds
    (5)   The Dues Year
    (6)   How Much Dues?
    (7)   Special Assessments
    (8)   Managing Dues Collection
    (9)   Dealing with Delinquents

(B)   A Treasurer's "Watch List"

(C)   Financial Reports to the Membership

(D)   Tax Concerns of Members

Chapter 7

Relations with the Membership

(A) Membership Dues

The primary source of income for most organizations is membership dues. For this reason, the treasurer should give careful consideration to the dues structure, not only when the organization is formed, but also throughout the organization's life. What may have been a satisfactory dues structure in the past may become obsolete through changing conditions.

(1) Who Sets the Dues?

To begin with, the responsibility for setting dues must be assigned either to the governing board or to the membership itself. Usually this is assigned to the governing board because it can make dues changes more quickly and easily than the membership as a whole. In fact, board discretion is almost a necessity where the membership is large and is reached primarily by mail. On the other hand, a small membership which holds regular meetings may wish to set its dues structure by a vote of the full membership rather than by a board of directors.

(2) Flat or Variable Dues

The body responsible for setting dues should make several key decisions before determining the dues amount. Will the dues be a flat figure per member, or will there be more than one dues rate? Dues can be made flexible by introducing multiple classes of membership based on any number of criteria.

Using membership classes can accomplish several objectives. Membership can be expanded by having a lower dues rate for a certain category of members, many of whom could not or would not pay the regular dues rate. Such classifications are often made available to students, retirees, low-income individuals, or recent entrants into an industry or profession. Low-cost memberships can also be made available to those desiring a reduced rate of benefits. For instance, country clubs often provide lower-cost social memberships to those desiring to use only the club restaurant and bar. A higher regular dues rate is charged to those using all club facilities, such as the golf course. On the other hand, some industry associations charge a regular rate for members of the industry and a higher rate for associate members who are not part of the industry, but who belong to the organization for the purpose of making sales to the industry. Of course, more than two classes of members can be used.

Variable dues, in addition to attracting members who would not otherwise join, may also serve the purpose of fairness, either with respect to ability to pay, use of benefits, or both. However, the sword is two-edged. Members willing to pay a single dues rate may be lost if put into a higher-priced category. The ability to pay a higher rate does not necessarily indicate a willingness to pay such a rate. Thus, introducing membership classes could actually make club income go down in certain circumstances if members at the high end of the dues scale drop out and are replaced only by those paying a special low rate.

(3)   Frequency of Dues Payment

As to the frequency of dues payment, an annual rate is most common by far. However, longer periods may be offered such as two years, four years, or life. Usually these are presented as alternatives to an annual rate, allowing the member to choose the most desirable duration. To make a longer period attractive, the price is usually less than the annual rate multiplied by the years involved. Even with this bargain element, the association can come out ahead by investing the money. The possibility of losing the member in the meantime is also avoided.

If an association considers offering a lifetime dues rate, the treasurer should caution the board against the common error of setting the lifetime dues rate too low. Inflation may soon force the organization to raise annual dues, with the result that lifetime dues payers will not be carrying their fair share of the load. As an alternative, the association can offer a reduced rate for a fixed number of years, such as five years for the price of four. This would protect the treasury against an undue loss of revenue over a long period.

Membership durations of less than a year are seldom used because of the extra record-keeping burden. There is always a certain percentage of the membership that will be delinquent in payment and require added collection efforts. These problems are doubled if semi-annual dues are adopted instead of annual dues. However, there is one exception. In some organizations new members are allowed to begin with a semi-annual or other short-period dues rate as an introductory offer. The idea is that prospective members may be reluctant to spend the whole annual fee before they have had a chance to try out the organization. A semi-annual payment for a trial period makes joining less of a risky proposition.

On the other hand, some associations, instead of giving new members a bargain, start them out with an initiation fee. Social and athletic clubs are good examples. Such organizations generally do not want a large membership growth. Instead, the initiation fee serves to pay for the extra costs of adding a member (providing them with materials, orientation, *etc.*) and also helps ensure that those joining will be serious members. The disruption and record-keeping burdens caused by members who join and then quickly resign are thereby avoided.

(4)   Dues Refunds

If a member leaves, will part of the annual dues be refunded? Some organizations do not allow refunds, whereas others do for specified causes (such as death or job transfers), and still others give all departing members a refund based on the remaining portion of the organization's year.

(5)   The Dues Year

Another issue is the billing cycle—the dues year. Will all members (except new ones) pay their dues at the beginning of the organization's year? Or will members pay their dues on the anniversary of their joining the organization? In the former case record-keeping is probably simplified, except that new members generally make an initial dues payment based on the portion of the organization's year that remains at the time they join. The latter alternative, the anniversary system, involves more record-keeping since up to 365 different billing dates must be monitored. However, this system does have the advantage of spreading out the task of billing evenly over the year rather than having a heavy workload when all the billing is done at once.

(6)   How Much Dues?

The level at which an organization sets the dues amount depends on its financial needs and desires. Some organizations set the dues to meet membership costs (such as periodicals, mailings and administrative expenses). Others try to cover the organization's entire cost through dues, sometimes after first reducing costs by subtracting other sources of revenue (such as sales, contributions and investment income). Others try to make a profit—often a substantial one—on dues. This is frequently done by charities and activist organizations.

The "profit," of course, goes to finance the organization's charitable or political programs.

A few organizations set dues at less than cost in order to attract as many members as possible. For instance, a political organization with plenty of other income can afford to provide a bargain dues rate. The idea is that the extra-large membership will give the organization more political clout. Or an organization that sells a substantial amount of advertising in its publication may reduce dues to increase the circulation of the publication, which in turn allows a higher rate to be charged to advertisers. This is similar to the strategy of many newspapers that price their paper at far below cost in order to maximize advertising revenue.

(7)   Special Assessments

Sometimes there is a miscalculation and the organization will run short of money. Some organizations in this situation attempt to make a special assessment, meaning that members are sent a bill asking for an additional payment above the amount of dues. Such assessments are often of doubtful value. Some members will be offended or feel cheated because they have to pay more to get what was promised when they paid their dues originally. Some members will not pay, and those who do pay will do so voluntarily. Since payments end up being voluntary anyway, it might be better just to solicit members for a contribution instead of trying to impose a special assessment. Another possibility is to borrow money to cover the shortfall and then increase the dues next year to pay off the loan.

(8)   Managing Dues Collection

The treasurer should monitor the rate at which dues are being collected and should report on this regularly to the governing body. A useful standard can be a comparison between the percentage of total dues billed that have been collected so far in the current year, and the percentage at a comparable date the previous year or years. Should there be a lag in dues payments, the treasurer can inquire into possible reasons and then recommend steps to overcome the deficiency.

Among the techniques used by various organizations to speed up dues payments are:

- Appealing for prompt payment through the association's periodical;
- Mailing second notices to members who have not paid;
- Sending personal notes to nonpayers, or making phone calls;

- Posting the names of delinquents on the clubhouse bulletin board or publishing the names in the association's periodical;

- Sending ultimatum letters specifying payment by a certain date to avoid cancellation of membership.

The effectiveness of these and other approaches to dues collection varies from one association to another, depending on their character and on the individuals concerned. One common method, which experience has shown does not work very well by itself, is to print the member's expiration date on the newsletter mailing label. Most people pay no attention to the mailing label unless they are reminded by some other form of contact. Since no single method works in every situation, the treasurer and executive body should follow the renewal procedure that best fits their own circumstances.

(9)   Dealing with Delinquents

A problem faced by all membership organizations in dues collection is that of delinquent members. Actually, there are three kinds of delinquent members: those who intend to drop out; those who intend to remain members but have neglected to pay their dues; and those who have not decided whether to continue membership. Each kind of delinquent member requires a different type of collection effort.

There is a common tendency to punish a delinquent member by assessing penalties, sending strongly-worded letters and threatening to drop the person from membership. The idea is to scare the member into promptly paying his dues. This strategy may work where the member has a definite need to belong to the organization. In many cases, however, the member does not really need the organization—a similar one may serve the same purpose, or the member can get along without any organization at all. Thus, the hard-line approach often backfires by alienating the delinquent member. Those intending to drop out anyway will not be persuaded, and those who are undecided are not given a positive incentive to decide favorably. Of those intending to renew, most would have eventually paid their dues without the scare tactic, and some may change their mind and not pay because of the negative approach.

Except in those rare instances where members definitely need and want this particular organization, the soft sell approach to collection is much better. Most nonprofit organizations realize that the best sources of dues and contributions are those who have paid dues or made contributions in the past. Therefore, repeated efforts should be made to contact delinquent members in an attempt to persuade them of the benefits of belonging to the organization. A combination of methods (letters, phone calls, reminders in newsletters, announcements at meetings) may be needed.

(B) A Treasurer's "Watch List"

From repeated incidents, the treasurer may sometimes identify a few association members who are not responsible about money. Such people may repeatedly write checks that are dishonored by their bank for insufficient funds. They may claim to have mailed a check for dues or tickets and it does not arrive. They may assert that they remember having paid when they have not. They may promise earnestly to pay later and must be reminded repeatedly to do so. If the association has a loan fund, they are among the first to borrow and the slowest to repay. The disease of financial irresponsibility seems to remain with such people and is not at all related to their ability to pay their way.

Unless such members are finally dropped from membership for nonpayment of dues, the treasurer is forced to cope with the difficulties they cause. One way is to send out word to the very few other people concerned, and in the most discreet manner possible, that all dealings with a particular member are to be on a strictly cash basis. For example, no extension of time for payment of anything should be permitted. Checks from that member are to be deposited promptly and a close watch should be kept on whether they are dishonored. The member should be kept at a distance from the association loan fund.

At the first irregularity after such a member is put on the discreet "watch list," the treasurer should see that a firm but courteous note is sent to the member pointing out the irregularity and asking immediate payment. The note should be completely objective in tone and should make it clear that the association must be run in a businesslike manner. Only when all else fails should the treasurer ask the executive body to take official action to recover money owed by a continually irresponsible member.

(C) Financial Reports to the Membership

Each organization should provide in its bylaws for a periodic treasurer's report to be made available to all members, usually on an annual basis. But if there are questions from members during the year between annual reports, such questions should normally be answered and any necessary supporting documentation should be supplied. As discussed in Chapter 3, the conscientious treasurer should be as open as possible in reporting to the membership on their association treasury. Except in special cases there is no reason for him to be secretive about it because in a democratically-run organization the members have a right to know how their money is being used.

At times the treasurer may encounter resistance to a policy of open access to financial information, particularly from another officer or governing board member. This person may think that certain pieces of financial bad news should be kept within the executive group and not let out to the membership at large. The treasurer should resist this line of thought. He can point out that his duty is to the membership as a whole, not merely to a leadership group. He can add that stating the financial facts candidly is much better for the organization than refusing to give out information because hiding the truth can lead to damaging rumors and dissatisfaction with the way the organization is being directed.

(D)   Tax Concerns of Members

The treasurer may be asked if dues are tax deductible. If all or a part of the dues are in fact donations for which the member receives nothing of value in return, and the organization is qualified to receive tax-deductible charitable contributions (Part II, R(1)), then members may take a deduction for the donation on their personal tax return if they itemize deductions.

If contributions are tax deductible, see Chapter 6(G) for information on the IRS-required statements which must be provided to donors if something is given to them in exchange for their contributions or if any contributions are $250.00 or larger.

If contributions are not tax deductible, see Part II, R(1) for the required notice of non-deductibility which must be sent out with any request for funds if the organization's annual gross receipts exceed $100,000.00.

Members who belong to the organization for a legitimate business reason may be able to deduct their dues as a business expense, even if a charitable contributions deduction is not allowed.

Chapter 8. DEALING WITH EMPLOYEES

(A)   Employer (Taxpayer) Identification Number

(B)   Salaries

(C)   Record of Earnings and Deductions

(D)   Non-Salary Benefits

(E)   Timely Payment

(F)   Advances on Salaries

(G)   Forms W-2 at Year-End

(H)   Encouraging Office Economies

(I)   The Employee Personnel File

(J)   Checklist for Hiring New Employees

(K)   References for Former Employees

(L)   Controlling Unemployment Claims

(M)   Non-Wage Payments and Expense Accounts

CHAPTER 8

Dealing with Employees

(A) Employer (Taxpayer) Identification Number

If an association has one or more employees or has investment income, it needs an identification number issued by the Internal Revenue Service, referred to as an Employer Identification Number or sometimes as a Taxpayer Identification Number. The number is needed to complete forms used when sending withheld wage taxes and FICA (Social Security) taxes to the IRS and withheld state income taxes to the state collection agency.

To obtain an identification number the association should obtain Form SS-4 ("Application for Employer Identification Number") from a local office of the IRS or the Social Security Administration and file it with the IRS. Few people in an association other than the treasurer ever use the number or even know there is such a thing. Therefore, after the assigned number is received, it is helpful to record it prominently in treasury folders devoted to payroll, taxes and any other relevant place so that an incoming treasurer or the office staff can easily find it. An outgoing treasurer should inform his successor where the number is recorded and how it is to be used.

(B) Salaries

As mentioned in Chapter 5, the treasurer should be among those who determine the salaries paid to employees because the cost of the salaried staff can be a major expense for the organization. The elements to consider in fixing a salary rate include these, among others:

- The prevailing rate being paid in the area for comparable work and skill;
- The salary necessary to attract a suitable employee;

- The amount necessary in the form of scheduled raises to retain a satisfactory employee; and

- The amount the association can afford to pay.

Frequently an association does not believe it can afford to pay a suitable employee what he or she is worth—particularly an executive secretary who is expected to run the office alone, or almost so. So the group may hire someone not up to the level required for the job and hope that with time the new employee will improve. Or it may fill the gap with a willing relative of a member who agrees to hold the fort until help arrives. Eventually, after such stop-gap employees have left or been asked to leave, the problem must be faced again.

The treasurer can play a valuable part in this process by presenting a realistic case for what he thinks the association can afford to pay for competent help. He may point out economies that would make it possible to employ a satisfactory person at a higher salary than was previously thought feasible. Or he may find a way to handle the work with fewer employees. Since money is at the root of the problem, the treasurer should be one of the decision-makers when an association hires employees and determines their salaries.

(C)   Record of Earnings and Deductions

When an association has one or more paid employees, the treasurer must see that it maintains an employee earnings record. Printed record forms that make the job easy can be bought at most stationery stores.

On every payday the treasurer should see that the earnings record of each employee is filled in for the pay period just ended. The record includes gross pay, each deduction for withheld federal income tax, FICA (Social Security), state and city taxes where applicable, other amounts withheld such as for insurance, the total of all deductions, and the net pay received by the employee. These individual records, when added together, show the total amounts due to the Internal Revenue Service for withheld income and FICA taxes, and to the state tax agency. When properly maintained, earnings records are evidence to an auditor that the association has been withholding the proper amounts from its employees' pay.

Record of Earnings and Deductions: All Employees

Employee's Name	Gross Pay	[— Deductions —]				Total Withheld	Net Pay
		Fed'l Income Tax Withheld	FICA Tax Withheld	State Income Tax Withheld	Insurance Withheld		
J. Doe	800.	160.	60.	40.	20.	280.	520.
R. Doe	600.	150.	45.	22.	17.	234.	366.
B. Nemo	500.	100.	37.50	16.	15.	168.50	331.50
This Payday	1,900.	410.	142.50	78.	52.	682.50	1,217.50

Record of Earnings and Deductions: J. Doe

	Gross Pay	[— Deductions —]				Total Withheld	Net Pay
		Fed'l Income Tax Withheld	FICA Tax Withheld	State Income Tax Withheld	Insurance Withheld		
1/15/XX	800.	160.	60.	40.	20.	280.	520.
1/29/XX	800.	160.	60.	40.	20.	280.	520.
2/12/XX	850.	170.	63.75	43.50	20.	297.25	552.75

When starting work, the new employee should be given a copy of his or her earnings and deductions schedule so that the difference between gross pay and net pay is made clear. Every time there is a change in the employee's gross pay or in a withholding rate, the treasurer should see that all employees affected receive a written statement of the new scale of deductions with the resulting net pay. If employees have questions about any deductions, the treasurer should see that they are answered.

Pay Schedule Notification

To: __(Employee name)__ :

    Below is your schedule of gross pay, weekly deductions and weekly net pay that you will receive in the coming fiscal year, starting with your paycheck of__(date)__ . If you have any questions, please bring them to the Association Treasurer.

Annual Pay Rate	26,000.
Weekly gross pay (26,000/52)	500.

DEDUCTIONS:

FEDERAL TAX	75.00
FICA (Social Security)	40.00
STATE TAX	24.50
Total Deductions	139.50

Net Weekly Pay	360.50

The treasurer should be alert to changes in withholding tax schedules, which sometimes accompany major tax legislation, and should learn where to obtain the federal, state and (if applicable) city tax tables showing the amount to be withheld at each wage level. Usually help is available from the taxing agency or from a law firm or certified public accountant. Federal information can be found on the Internet at http://www.irs.gov.

(D)   Non-Salary Benefits

Just as the treasurer should take part in setting the salaries paid to association employees, he should also be involved in establishing the program of non-salary benefits. The reason is that he is in the best position to help the governing board get a realistic picture of the full cost of each employee and of what non-salary benefits the association can afford. Hospitalization and other health insurance costs paid by the employer can be the most expensive benefits. One way to control their cost is by making them contributory, with part of the premiums paid by the employee. (This may also cause employees to better appreciate the benefit.) An annual bonus, whether given at Christmastime or at the end of the fiscal year, can be kept to a modest level. But it can become an albatross around the organization's neck if it becomes a routine expected cash gift that is not related to an employee's effort. And it is difficult to terminate without causing bad feelings.

MEMORANDUM

TO: Executive Board

DATE: 2/14/XX

FROM: Treasurer

SUBJ: Cost of Proposed Additional Employee, Salary and Benefits

The full cost to the association of hiring an employee is frequently underestimated because non-salary benefits are not taken fully into account. The table below shows how much the proposed additional employee would cost the association when benefits are added to the salary.

The calculation of days actually worked is provided in order to give a true picture of time worked in relation to salary-plus-benefits cost. Time off from work does not entail expenditure except as it may lead to hiring short-term people to catch up with the work load.

Employee's annual salary		$26,000
FICA tax on salary (rounded)		1,950
Christmas bonus (traditional)		100
Hospitalization insurance ($100 per month)		1,200
Benefits total		3,250 (12-1/2% of payroll)
Total, salary plus benefits		$29,250

Calculation of days worked:

Total days in year, excl. Sat. And Sun.			261
Days not worked:			
Vacation		15	
Holidays, incl. compensating days off for weekend holidays	10		
Illness, emergencies (estimated)	(0 - 10)		
	25 - 35		
Days worked (with variation for illness)			236-226

The most economical benefit to employees, and one which most associations can arrange, is time off from work. Unless there are association events tied to certain dates that make it impossible, the organization can usually afford to be generous with scheduled holidays and with vacations taken during slack periods. In most cases a conscientious office staff member gets the necessary work done before and after holidays, and plans to take vacations when the office work is caught up. Of course, the treasurer and other officers should see that the holidays/vacation policy is consistent with getting the necessary work done.

(E) Timely Payment

The treasurer should see that association employees are paid strictly on time. If he cannot be available to sign salary checks so that they reach employees on the scheduled payday, he should make arrangements for someone else to do so. There are occasions when a volunteer officer is casual about making timely payment, without thinking that an employee may have counted on receiving the paycheck in order to make a necessary purchase or to cover personal checks already written. The treasurer would certainly not stand for such casualness on the part of his own employer, so he should not be thoughtless about paying the association staff when their pay is due. If the employees have done their work during the pay period, they have a right to their money on schedule.

(F) Advances on Salaries

On occasion a staff employee may approach the treasurer with a hard-luck story about needing an advance payment of salary to meet an emergency at home. When this occurs, the treasurer should remember that he is in a position of trust with control over other people's money.

Except in rare and special cases, the treasurer should not pay an employee in advance from association funds. One reason is that the "emergency" may become a habit, especially if the importuning employee sees the treasurer as a soft touch. Once started, such a habit may be difficult to break and embarrassing if the borrower and treasurer are particularly friendly. Another reason is that anyone—another employee or a member—may become suspicious of the relationship between borrower and treasurer and may question the honesty of the transaction. No treasurer should court suspicion in this way.

However, if the treasurer is convinced that there is a genuine emergency and if the reason for the advance seems compelling, he should protect himself by asking the president or another officer to approve it.

(G) Forms W-2 at Year-End

At the end of the calendar year, the treasurer should see that an IRS Form W-2 ("Wage and Tax Statement") is filled out for each employee, showing the gross pay during the year and the amount withheld for each category of federal and state tax. To prepare this form without undue difficulty, it is essential that an employee earnings record be kept faithfully. Without it, the treasurer would have a difficult time reconstructing the annual totals if there has been any change in salary during the year, or overtime pay, or other complication. One copy of Form W-2 should be kept in the association files, one sent to the Social Security Administration by the end of the following February, one sent to the state tax agency (if applicable), and the other copies should be given to all employees by January 31 for use in preparing their income tax returns. If a person resigns or is discharged during the year, a Form W-2 must be provided to the person within 30 days if requested.

If payments are made to workers who are not employees, see Chapters 6(E) and 8(M) for the tax reporting requirements.

(H) Encouraging Office Economies

Because he is likely to be the most cost-conscious officer of an association, and because he is frequently in a position to observe employees at work, the treasurer can play a major role in controlling office costs. He can establish standards that save money almost daily by setting a good example himself and by pointing out to the staff ways in which waste can be avoided. A few examples:

- Telephone—he can keep the calls he makes from the association office brief and to the point and avoid chatting at long-distance rates. He can also appeal to the office staff, particularly to the person in charge, to follow his example, making it clear that personal visiting on the office telephone is not one of the perquisites of the job.

- Copying machine—he can limit the number of his copies to only those that he needs and encourage the staff to avoid running off extra copies that are discarded later.

- Stationery—he can encourage the association to purchase in sensible quantities, and to avoid over-buying printed items that will be useless later because the office address or officers' names are out of date.

- Messengers—he can encourage the consolidation of deliveries to the bank, printer and other places to save messenger service costs. He can also switch in some cases from messengers to the U.S. Postal Service where delivery by messenger is not really necessary.

(I) The Employee Personnel File

Even in the smallest association, the treasurer should make sure that a personnel file is created for each employee. At a minimum, the following items should be kept in the file:

(1) Employment application, if any.

(2) Age and other background information needed for the association's pension and insurance programs, if any.

(3) The employee's salary history with the association, showing the current rate of pay and the dates and amounts of previous raises. This information is especially helpful to successor treasurers, not only in preparing the payroll, but also in determining the amount and timing of future raises.

(4) IRS Form W-4 signed by the employee showing the number of exemptions claimed for wage withholding purposes.

(5) Form I-9 issued by the Immigration and Naturalization Service showing proof of legal residence for employees hired after November 6, 1986. While many small associations will probably ignore this law (if they are aware of it at all), nonetheless it is a requirement.

(6) If used by the association, any written job descriptions and performance evaluations.

The personnel file should be retained at least four years after the person's employment has ended.

(J)   Checklist for Hiring New Employees

Evaluating applicants' qualifications and deciding whom to hire is normally beyond the scope of the treasurer's function. However, the treasurer may be involved in certain administrative aspects of hiring and should be aware of the following:

(1)   Employment Application and Interview.

To minimize the risk of discrimination lawsuits, the treasurer should mainly be aware of information that applicants must <u>not</u> provide prior to the hiring decision. This includes any personal information that is not relevant to performance of the particular job, including age, sex, race, religion, national origin, marital status, number of children, ages of children, and any handicaps that do not prevent performance of the task (for instance, blindness might be a barrier to a jet pilot's position, but not to an association executive's position). Of course, some of these matters may be obvious by simple observation (a person's sex, for instance), but the employment application itself must not ask for them, nor may applicants be specifically asked such questions during any pre-hiring interview.

Beware of using old employment application forms which may still be on hand or purchased from an office supply store. Sometimes they still contain some of the above prohibited questions.

(2)   Post-hiring Matters

After an applicant is hired, the association needs to obtain some of the above personal information for insurance, tax and other purposes—which is acceptable since the previous hiring decision presumably would not have been made for these reasons. The treasurer should consider the following matters:

- With respect to information about age, children, *etc.*, as needed for insurance purposes, this can be submitted on a separate post-hiring form, or some establishments ask for it on a separate section of the employment application which instructs applicants to avoid this part unless and until they are hired. Or successful applicants can fill out the necessary group insurance forms themselves and submit them to the association for further processing.

- All new employees must fill out IRS Form W-4 to show the number of exemptions and marital status they are claiming for tax withholding purposes. (If individuals want to claim fewer exemptions than they are entitled to, or if married persons wish to declare themselves single, this is acceptable to the IRS since such steps only increase the amount of withholding.)

- All employees must fill out Form I-9 for the Immigration and Naturalization Service, establishing their right to work in the United States.

- The federal Department of Labor (and any corresponding state agency) should be contacted about the prevailing minimum wage and overtime pay requirements.

(K)   References for Former Employees

This is an increasingly tricky business where the former employee was incompetent, dishonest or dangerous. Of course, giving a bad reference (even if accurate) could trigger a defamation lawsuit or civil rights complaint against both you and the association by the former employee. Recently, however, former employers have also been sued by the next employer where they gave good references for former employees who proved to be disasters at the new job. This is particularly true where the former employee had dishonest or dangerous propensities. Even merely confirming the former employee's employment dates while remaining silent about such propensities could lead to a lawsuit. In this Catch-22 situation, the only safe courses of action are to obtain legal advice or to simply say, "No comment, period," without even confirming that the person had ever been an employee.

Of course, there is usually no harm in giving a good, accurate recommendation for a former employee who performed satisfactorily.

(L)   Controlling Unemployment Claims

The association needs to be concerned about unemployment compensation claims of former employees since this causes the association's unemployment tax rate to increase in the future.

If a claim is filed, the association has a short time period in which to contest it. During this contest period and any appeals, there will be several deadlines which the association may have to meet for filing notices or documents. All such deadlines must be strictly complied with. Being late by even one day could cause the association to have its contest disallowed. Also, it is important to provide all relevant documents and testimony at the first hearing—attempts to bring up new information at a later date or during appeals probably will be denied.

A contest should be considered whenever the employee voluntarily quits or was terminated for committing a dishonest act, violating a significant work rule, or disobeying a specific job instruction. Unless the violation is flagrant or dishonest, the employer's case is strongest when the employee's behavior persists after two written warnings. On the other hand, it is difficult to contest a claim where the employee was terminated because his job was eliminated, or the association could not afford him, or the person tried in good faith to do his job but simply did not perform well enough.

Documentation is essential to support a valid claim contest. Important work rules should be in writing and given to employees when hired. Employee violations or warnings should be recorded promptly and kept in the personnel file with a copy handed to the employee at that time.

(M)   Non-Wage Payments and Expense Accounts

Chapter 6(E) discusses the tax reporting requirements for payments made to a person not an employee. Generally Form 1099-MISC must be filed with the IRS when the person is paid $600.00 or more annually. That section also discusses how to distinguish between an employee and a worker who is not treated as an employee. Examples of non-employee workers usually include those providing lawn care, snow plowing, catering, entertainment, seminar instruction, and paid banquet speaking.

Not only is the tax reporting different for employees versus non-employees, as discussed in Chapter 6, but the responsibility for paying taxes is also different. Employees have required amounts of income and FICA taxes withheld. Non-employees, on the other hand, have no withholding and have to make their own arrangements to pay the IRS both for income taxes and for the self-employed version of FICA tax. This should be made clear to anyone paid on a non-employee basis unless it is obvious that the person already knows about the tax responsibilities.

All too often an association will pay someone such as a retired person, say, $5,000.00 for part-time help around the office or with special projects, and the person (who may be accustomed to just getting a "net" paycheck with all taxes withheld) doesn't realize that the $5,000.00 is not totally "free and clear." Perhaps the entire $5,000.00 will be spent before the person's tax return is prepared. Then the person discovers too late that perhaps up to $2,000.00 in taxes must be paid on the $5,000.00. The treasurer should warn such a person about this potential problem.

With respect to expense reimbursements, if the reimbursement is only for the exact amount of expenses actually incurred, and detailed records are retained either by the person or by the association (and any payment for mileage does not exceed the current IRS allowance—36 cents per mile in 2003), then the reimbursement does not need to be reported to the IRS and no withholding needs to be made, regardless of whether the person is an employee or a non-employee.

However, if the person is paid a fixed expense allowance or auto allowance (such as $100.00 per month), then this is treated as taxable compensation. For employees, this amount is added to wage payments on Form W-2 and the appropriate tax withholdings must be made. For non-employees, the amount is shown on Form 1099-MISC if the person is paid $600.00 or more annually (including any other compensation paid by the association). In either case, as an offset against this income, recipients should then attempt to deduct on their personal tax returns some or all of the expenses they actually incurred.

PART II

A.   Forming a New Organization 107

B.   Obtaining and Retaining Tax-exempt Status 114

C.   Payroll Taxes 125

D.   Checklist of Reports and Payments 131

E.   Single or Double Entry Bookkeeping? 135

F.   Cash or Accrual Method? 138

G.   Blocking Frauds and Theft 144

H.   Finding Errors 149

I.   Preparing the Annual Financial Report 152

J.   Handling the IRS Audit 161

K.   Change of Association's Name 170

L.   Changing the Association Financial System 172

M.   Using Computers 175

N.   Using Bank Payroll Services 179

O.   Unrelated Business Income Tax 181

P.   Fund Accounting 189

Q.   Private Foundations 195

R.   Charitable Contributions 199

A. FORMING A NEW ORGANIZATION

(1)   Corporate or Noncorporate?

(2)   Place of Organization

(3)   Name

(4)   Management of the Organization

(5)   Articles of Incorporation

(6)   Bylaws

(7)   Annual Duties

(8)   Other Permits and Exemptions

A.   Forming a New Organization

The legal mechanics of setting up a nonprofit organization can be quite simple. First, several key decisions must be made, such as the legal form of the organization, its purpose, its name, its location, its membership and its management. Once these hurdles are cleared, the rest is easy. If the corporate form is chosen, the articles of incorporation are filed with the state, an incorporation fee is paid, an initial meeting is held, bylaws are adopted, an application for tax-exempt status may be filed with the IRS, and presto, the nonprofit organization is under way. While creating the organization occasionally can be complex, most situations are not. Laymen sometimes perform all these steps without the assistance of a lawyer. However, in most cases having the services of a lawyer is advisable. The cost of a few hundred dollars in legal fees is small compared to the damage which can be caused by a defective incorporation or the loss of tax-exempt status.

(1)   Corporate or Noncorporate?

The first decision is whether to form the organization as a corporation or as some other type of entity, such as a trust, partnership or unincorporated association. Usually a corporation is preferable. For instance, a corporation can provide limited liability to some extent; members and others involved in the organization usually would not be personally liable for debts or negligence on the part of the organization. On the other hand, the participants in a partnership or unincorporated association are often personally liable for the organization's debts and could be personally sued for the organization's misconduct.

Corporations also have the capability of unlimited life. The legal entity can continue in existence even after all the original members and directors are gone.

Finally, a corporation may hold property, such as real estate, in its own name. This is important from a convenience standpoint; in some states, an unincorporated association is not allowed to own property in its own name. In this situation the real estate would then have to be held in the name of each individual member, making a later sale of the property difficult if not impossible.

(2)   Place of Organization

The next step is selecting the state in which the organization will be incorporated. In most cases the local state is the best bet. Although one sometimes hears that a particular state—such as Delaware—is more desirable for incorporation, any advantages of a non-local state are usually exaggerated. In extreme circumstances using the laws of a non-local state may be important, but usually not. Modern state corporation laws are now similar in most respects, and use of a non-local state can cause many inconveniences. A non-local lawyer probably will have to be hired, and registration as a foreign corporation in the local state may be necessary. Filing fees and annual report fees could be doubled for this reason. Finally, amending the articles of incorporation in future years may be more difficult because the filing must be made in another state.

(3)   Name

The next step is to select the name of the organization. From a legal standpoint, almost any name may be chosen so long as it is not the same as or deceptively similar to the name of another corporation registered in the state. Sometimes the corporate name must also contain the abbreviations "Inc.," "Assn.," "Co.," or "Ltd." to identify the entity as a corporation. Of course, as a practical matter, a name should be selected that satisfies various non-legal objectives such as describing the organization, getting attention, and being easy to remember. The local Secretary of State's office can be contacted to determine whether the desired name is available.

(4)   Management of the Organization

Who will be the organization's incorporators? Who will be on the initial board of directors? How will replacements be selected? These questions must be answered before the organization is formed.

Incorporators serve no purpose except to list their names on the articles of incorporation as "sponsors" of the organization. No work of any kind is required. In many states only one individual is required; other states require three. Often the individuals must reside in the state of incorporation. Usually members of the initial board of directors serve as the incorporators.

More important than selecting the incorporators is selecting the directors (sometimes called trustees). Unlike incorporators, directors have continuing duties and authority. Directors generally are not involved in detailed day-to-day management. However, they often elect officers and establish the broad operating rules and policies of the organization. Again, some states allow a corporation to have only one director while others require three. In some states directors must also be residents.

Should more than the minimum number of directors be used? This depends on the needs and desires of each organization.

Many organizations prefer a large number of directors for several reasons. A large number can help keep the organization from being controlled by one person or a small clique. Having business and professional persons as directors can also provide a source of free advice on financial, legal, management, fundraising and other matters. Usually the organization would have to pay dearly to purchase these professional services, but many business persons will donate their time and ideas in exchange for the public relations value and social status of being the director of a community organization. Similarly, making directorships available to large contributors is a good way to keep those contributors loyal. Finally, having the names of prominent individuals on the board gives the organization prestige and credibility, which is especially important for a new organization. This, in turn, makes it easier for the organization to get loans, grants, contracts, and above all, contributions from the public. When most people receive a solicitation in the mail, they look for familiar names on the letterhead. One or two recognizable names can sometimes mean the difference between mailing a contribution or throwing the solicitation away. Directors are valuable not only for this, but they may even act as fundraisers with their employees, clients and other business contacts.

On the other hand, having a large number of directors can make meetings more difficult to schedule. Arriving at decisions can also be a drawn-out process because there may be added discussion and dissension. The organization must therefore balance the benefits of a large number of directors against the disadvantages when determining the size of the board.

One last word about the number of directors: Usually an odd number is chosen to avoid the problem of tie votes.

Once the number of directors has been set (either as a simple number or as a range between a minimum and a maximum), the next question is how to select them. The initial members of the board are named in the articles of incorporation. Directors thereafter are chosen by either member election or an election within the board itself. Most organizations have a membership which is used as the electoral body. However, certain organizations such as colleges and private foundations may have no membership. In this situation the board itself will elect replacements whenever a director leaves. Such a board, of course, tends to be self-perpetuating.

A third possibility, in the case of a subsidiary or auxiliary organization, is for the directors of the subsidiary to be chosen by the board of the parent.

The terms of the directors must also be specified in the articles. One year is the most common duration, although any length of time, such as two years or four years, may be used. Directors may also be elected for an indefinite term, serving until their death or resignation.

(5) Articles of Incorporation

Once the decisions have been made regarding the name, location and directors of the organization, the articles of incorporation can be prepared. This is usually a simple task as most articles are no more than half a dozen pages long. Many, if not all, of the provisions can be copied out of a legal forms book.

Generally, the articles should set forth the organization's name, address, registered agent (a person designated to represent the corporation at its official address), duration (usually perpetual), incorporators, initial directors, election procedures, purposes, powers, recipients of assets upon liquidation, and whether or not there is a corporate seal (having a seal is usually optional).

If income tax exempt status is desired, the following clauses are important:

▸ Purpose—This must conform to the requirements for the type of exempt status desired (Part II(B)(1)(c)).

▸ Powers—This clause must limit the legal powers of the organization to those of a nonprofit nature. In addition, the clause usually contains boilerplate language allowing the corporation to invest funds, obtain loans, convey real estate, and so forth.

▸ Inurement—The articles of most nonprofit organizations must provide that assets cannot be used for the benefit of (or "inure" to) a private party (Part II(B)(2)(d)).

▸ Liquidation—For most nonprofit organizations, this clause must provide that if the organization is dissolved, all assets are turned over to another nonprofit entity.

The articles are then signed by the incorporators, notarized, and filed with the Secretary of State and sometimes the county recorder, together with the incorporation fee.

(6) Bylaws

Once the state has issued a certificate of incorporation, an initial meeting of the directors can be held. The most important task here is adopting a set of bylaws. These provide the organization with a written set of operating guidelines, going into more detail than the articles.

Again, while the bylaws may be lengthy—perhaps up to twenty pages—most provisions can be copied from a legal forms book. Generally, the bylaws cover the qualifications of members, the duties of officers, the dues structure, the permissible uses of funds, the allowable investments, and the manner of making amendments.

(7)   Annual Duties

Once the organization is started, little is necessary to keep it legally in existence. Directors' meetings should be held at least once a year to avoid charges that the corporation has become defunct. Even if there is nothing to discuss, a brief meeting should still be held at which officers are reelected and their actions during the past year approved. Minutes of each meeting should be recorded.

Another small but essential duty is the filing of an annual report with the state of incorporation, usually in the office of Secretary of State. Generally the report consists of just a few questions such as the names of officers and directors. A nominal fee is also required. If the report is not filed, the corporate charter may be canceled, meaning that officers and directors could become personally liable for the organization's debts or negligent activities.

Besides failing to hold meetings or file an annual report, an organization can also have its charter canceled for serious violations of the state nonprofit corporation law. For instance, such laws typically provide that organization funds cannot be used for the benefit of a private party, such as an officer withdrawing large amounts for personal use in excess of a reasonable salary.

(8)   Other Permits and Exemptions

A new organization should also be aware of the following permits it may be required to obtain, or exemptions it should apply for:

(a)   Permits

- ▸ *Sales Tax:* If the organization sells anything, the state revenue department should be contacted about sales tax requirements.

- ▸ *Solicitations:* If the organization solicits donations, the local Secretary of State and the city clerk should be contacted about any relevant licenses.

- ▸ *Employee Matters:* If the organization has paid employees, the state revenue department and state unemployment bureau should be contacted about initial registration for employers.

- ▸ *Specific Functions:* If the organization obtains funds from food, liquor, gambling, second-hand sales or other regulated matters, the relevant state or local agency should be contacted for current requirements.

- ▸ *Catch-all:* To help make sure your organization has all required licenses and permits, you should contact the offices of the secretary of state and the city clerk and tell them about the nature of your new organization. Also, many states have a "one-stop" information center for new businesses, usually connected with the state economic development bureau, which can provide such information to you.

(b) Exemptions

▸ *Sales Taxes:* In some states, certain nonprofit organizations are exempt. Contact the state revenue department for further details.

▸ *Property Taxes:* Likewise, in some states you may be exempt from certain property taxes. Contact the county treasurer or assessor for details.

▸ *Postage Rates:* Certain tax-exempt organizations may apply for lower postage rates. Also, any establishment can obtain reduced postage rates for bulk or presorted mail. Contact your post office for information.

B. OBTAINING AND RETAINING TAX-EXEMPT STATUS

(1)   Obtaining Tax-Exempt Status
     (a)   Employer Identification Number
     (b)   Pros and Cons of Tax-Exempt Status
     (c)   Procedure to Obtain Exempt Status
     (d)   Annual Reporting

(2)   Retaining Tax-Exempt Status
     (a)   Misstatements in Application
     (b)   Discontinuing Exempt Activities
     (c)   Excessive Unrelated Activities
     (d)   Giving Benefits to Private Persons
     (e)   Political Activities
     (f)   Discrimination

B. Obtaining and Retaining Tax-Exempt Status

(1) Obtaining Tax-Exempt Status

(a) Employer Identification Number

One of the first things the treasurer of a new organization should do is apply for an Employer Identification Number from the IRS on Form SS-4. In earlier years some small organizations without paid employees did not obtain such a number, but under present law an identification number is needed to have a bank account or to own stocks and bonds. Thus, in most cases, the new organization should apply for a number at once.

(b) Pros and Cons of Tax-Exempt Status

The treasurer of a new organization must also address the question of whether the organization will be taxable or tax-exempt. The most obvious advantage of tax-exempt status is the privilege of not paying income taxes. However, this privilege is not complete—income taxes may still be owed on "unrelated business income" (Part II(O)). Furthermore, the organization may be subject to a variety of excise taxes on private foundations (Part II(Q)), to payroll taxes (Part II(C)), and to state and local property and sales taxes.

The second major advantage of tax-exempt status is the ability of the organization's donors to obtain a charitable contributions deduction under certain circumstances. Not all exempt organizations have this ability—generally only those exempt under section 501(c)(3) and (19) do (Part II(R)(1)).

Disadvantages of exempt status include the cost and paperwork required to obtain IRS approval, together with the extra restrictions placed on the organization's operation due to its special status.

Generally, most charities or associations choose tax-exempt status. However, there are a few circumstances where non-exempt (taxable) status is actually better. Such situations include:

> ▸ Where the organization will perpetually operate at the break-even point or at a loss. Since there would be no tax regardless of status, the extra paperwork in obtaining exempt status may not be worthwhile (assuming that tax-deductible contributions will not be solicited).

> ▸ Where the organization does not plan to operate as an exempt entity for a long period. An exempt organization switching to taxable status

or going out of business may be worse off than if taxable status had been used all along. Reasons for this include restrictions, paperwork and penalty taxes.

(c) Procedure to Obtain Exempt Status

Once the decision to obtain tax-exempt status has been made, the next step is determining the exemption category into which the organization will fall. The primary categories are as follows:

▸ Section 501(c)(3): Religious, charitable, scientific, literary, educational, testing for public safety, fostering amateur sports competition.

▸ Section 501(c)(4): Civic leagues.

▸ Section 501(c)(5): Labor unions, agricultural associations.

▸ Section 501(c)(6): Business leagues, trade associations, chambers of commerce.

▸ Section 501(c)(7): Social or recreational clubs.

▸ Section 501(c)(8): Fraternal insurance programs.

▸ Section 501(c)(9): Voluntary employees' beneficiary associations.

▸ Section 501(c)(10): Fraternities and lodges.

▸ Section 501(c)(19): War veterans organizations.

▸ Section 527: Political organizations.

▸ Section 521: Agricultural cooperatives.

▸ Section 528: Homeowners associations.

▸ Section 501(c)(2): A title-holding company which turns all profits over to another exempt organization.

In addition to falling into one of the above categories, an organization generally must refrain from participating in political campaigns, must refrain from racial discrimination, and generally must not allow any of its earnings to be used for the benefit of a private individual.

This last requirement precludes investment clubs and similar profit-oriented entities from obtaining exempt status where distributions can be made to the owners. Such entities must operate as a partnership or as a taxable corporation.

Application for exempt status is made on Form 1023 for 501(c)(3) organizations, or on Form 1024 for most other organizations. Churches do not need to file for exemption. Section 501(c)(3) organizations (other than churches) should file the application form within 15 months after the date of incorporation.

The law now requires that applications for tax exemption be accompanied by Form 8718 together with payment of a "user fee." Presently the user fee is $500.00, except for organizations expected to average $10,000.00 or less of annual gross receipts over their first four years, in which case the fee is $150.00. Form 8718 should be consulted for the latest fee schedule. It can be found on the Internet at: www.irs.gov.

No matter how carefully the application for exemption is prepared, usually the IRS will want more information before the application is approved. Unfortunately, the IRS request for further information tends to be a bit abrupt, sometimes informing the organization that its application is "denied" and that the IRS will assume that the organization does not wish to pursue the application further unless you contact them within a certain number of days. Don't be alarmed. This type of IRS response is common, and so long as you provide the additional information within the stated time period, often the so-called "denied" application will be "approved." (If you can't provide the information within the stated time period, contact the IRS promptly and request an extension of time.)

A copy of the application for tax exemption and the IRS letter approving it must be kept available for public inspection during normal business hours. The names and addresses of donors may be deleted from the copy open to inspection. For further information on public disclosure requirements, see Chapter 6(H).

(d) *Annual Reporting*

All tax-exempt organizations (other than churches) must concern themselves with the requirements for filing annual tax returns with the IRS, even if no tax is owed.

A tax-exempt organization (other than a private foundation) does not need to file a return for the current year if it meets one of the following conditions:

(1) It is one year or less old and received (or was pledged) less than $37,500.00 in its first year.

(2) It is between one and three years old and averaged $30,000.00 or less in total receipts during its first two years.

(3) It is three or more years old and averaged $25,000.00 or less in total receipts during the last three years.

These complicated conditions can be simplified to the following rule of thumb: If the organization received less than $25,000.00 in each of the last four years, no return needs to be prepared. Because of severe monetary penalties for not filing a return if it is required, though, the treasurer should be very sure that the organization meets the conditions for not filing. If in doubt, the treasurer should either get professional advice, such as from a CPA, or should file a return just to be safe. There is usually no harm, other than the loss of time, in filing a return that is not required.

If returns were previously filed and then the organization stops filing because it meets the above conditions, expect to get a brusque letter from the IRS inquiring about the absent returns. This then necessitates a letter in response explaining why no return was required. The organization can avoid this by continuing to file returns, but checking a box (currently Box K) on the front page so that no dollar amounts need to be filled in. The return is blank except for the name, address and identification number at the top and signature at the end.

If a return is required or will be filed even if not required, the next step is to determine what form to use. Usually this is Form 990 (or 990-EZ in lieu of 990 as discussed below). For these forms, the due date is the 15th day of the fifth month after year-end (May 15th in the case of a calendar-year organization). However, political organizations file Form 1120-POL; cooperatives file Form 990-C; and private foundations file Form 990-PF (Part II(Q)(3)).

Non-exempt partnerships file Form 1065, which is due by the 15th day of the fourth month following year-end. Non-exempt corporations, on the other hand, file Form 1120 which is due on the 15th day of the third month.

Where a Form 990 would otherwise be filed, if the organization received less than $100,000.00 during the current year and has less than $250,000.00 in assets at the end of the year, then it may file Form 990-EZ instead. As indicated by the "EZ," it is "easy" (two pages) compared to a regular Form 990 (six pages). However, if because of a lack of an EZ Form or doubt about the EZ requirements or the desire to be consistent with prior years, the treasurer can always file Form 990 even when an EZ would suffice.

Regardless of whether a Form 990 or 990-EZ is filed, if the organization is tax-exempt under Internal Revenue Code section 501(c)(3) (and is not a church), it must also fill out and attach a tax form called Schedule A (six pages) to the 990 or 990-EZ. Schedule B is also required to list donors who contributed $5,000.00 or more during the year.

For organizations exempt under sections 501(c)(7), (8), or (9), Schedule B may also be required for donors contributing more than $1,000.00 during the year.

In addition to the forms mentioned above, the organization sometimes has to file a comparable report with the state government. Still other state forms may be necessary for an annual franchise fee which keeps the corporate charter in good standing or to comply with reporting requirements if you solicit donations. These rules and forms vary from state to state, and an attorney or CPA should be consulted if the treasurer is unfamiliar with the requirements.

Where federal tax returns cannot be completed by the due date, an extension should be obtained ahead of time by filing Form 8868. Failure to file either the return or an Form 8868 by the due date usually results in penalties which accumulate at the rate of $20.00 or more per day. Thus, letting a few months slip by can lead to hundreds of dollars in penalties—even if the return is for a small organization which owes no tax.

Returns may also be necessary for payroll taxes at both the federal and state levels (Part II(C)(4)), and for taxes on unrelated business income (Part II(O)(4)).

When filing for an extension on Form 8868, an initial extension for three months is allowed automatically (assuming you filed Form 8868 on time) and no reason needs to be be given. This would give you a revised due date of August 15th for organizations using a calendar year. If still more time is needed, a second three-month extension can be applied for on Form 8868 (again, the form must be filed before the first revised due date—August 15th for calendar-year organizations) but this time you need to give an acceptable reason. The IRS states that vague reasons such as "busy" or "sick" will not be accepted. Your authors' experience, however, indicates that most specific reasons are approved. One reason that has always worked for your authors (but is not guaranteed to work for you) is "more time is needed to complete the accounting records in order to prepare an accurate return." Of course, if there is a better reason, such as illness of the treasurer or a fire, theft or death, this should be described in detail.

No further extensions of time (beyond the first two extensions mentioned above) are available, so a return MUST be filed before the second extension expires. Just do the best you can with whatever information you have, even if it is less than perfect.

When filing an extension request or the tax return itself, a copy should always be retained, and it is advisable to obtain proof of filing in one of two ways. If you are near an IRS office, the form can be hand delivered to the IRS and your copy file-stamped "Received" at that time. Alternatively, you can send the form to the IRS by certified mail, obtaining a stamped mailing receipt at the post office window. This may seem like an unnecessary effort, but it protects your organization against getting a computer notice from the IRS months later claiming that no form was filed and that substantial penalties are due. Even if the form was filed, such computer notices have been sent, and you may be unable to prove the filing without a file-stamped copy or certified mail receipt.

If penalties are assessed against the organization and timely filing cannot be proved, the only way to avoid the penalties is to demonstrate "reasonable cause." Generally this is only an unavoidable disaster such as fire or theft, or an officer's death or illness. However, even if good reasons such as these are not available, sometimes it is worthwhile to contest substantial penalties, and professional assistance may be desirable.

If your organization is tax-exempt, copies of any annual federal tax returns (usually Forms 990 or 990-PF) filed for the last three years must be kept available for public inspection during normal business hours. The names and addresses of donors may be deleted from the copies open for inspection. For further information on public disclosure requirements, *see* Chapter 6(H). Updated information on these matters is at: www.irs.gov.

(2)　Retaining Tax-Exempt Status

Obtaining exempt status is not the last tax hurdle your organization has to face—it is only the first. Exempt status can be revoked at any time if the organization engages in certain acts. While losing exempt status does not happen frequently, the consequences can be catastrophic. The organization's income is taxed, of course, but this is not all. Donors can no longer get a charitable contributions deduction which, together with the adverse publicity which usually accompanies revocation, means that the organization will not attract any more donations. Preferential treatment may also be lost in the areas of payroll taxes, property taxes and postage rates.

Exempt status may be lost for one of the following reasons:

- ▸ Misstatements in the exempt status application
- ▸ Discontinuing exempt activities
- ▸ Excessive unrelated activities
- ▸ Giving benefits to private persons
- ▸ Certain political activities
- ▸ Racial or other discrimination

To discuss these topics in more detail:

(a)　*Misstatements in Application*

If the organization makes a significant misstatement or omission in its application for exempt status, the IRS may revoke the exemption <u>retroactively</u> upon discovering the mistake. This means that the organization is not only taxable in the current and future years, but that taxes will also be assessed for all prior years as well. Minor mistakes such as an incorrect zip code would not produce this result—but mistakes in describing powers or restrictions contained in the organization's articles of incorporation could be critical.

(b) *Discontinuing Exempt Activities*

Obviously, if an organization discontinues all or nearly all its exempt activities, tax-free status could be in jeopardy. This does not mean that an organization cannot reduce the scale of its activities because of financial problems or other conditions—the danger arises only if the organization becomes inactive or carries on at most a trivial amount of exempt operations. However, there could also be problems if the organization changes from one type of exempt activity to a completely different type of exempt activity. An organization is usually granted tax-free status for only a limited range of functions and does not have an open license to roam far and wide across the spectrum of all exempt activities. For instance, an association of car dealers probably couldn't just convert to an association of travel agents on the spur of the moment. Making a successful switch could require amendment of the organization's charter and probably IRS permission. Even if the organization didn't lose its exemption, a switch might cause exempt status to be "downgraded" to a less favorable section number. Thus, an exempt trade school which converted into a trade association might still be exempt, but now under section 501(c)(6) instead of 501(c)(3). Exempt status here has been downgraded since payments to a section 501(c)(6) organization are not deductible as charitable contributions.

(c) *Excessive Unrelated Activities*

Exempt status may also be lost if the organization, while conducting plenty of exempt activities, nonetheless conducts an excessive amount of unrelated business activities (Part II(O)(1)). However, with one exception, there is no mathematical ratio defining what is "excessive." A general rule of thumb, though, is that so long as exempt activities predominate, tax-free status is probably safe. On the other hand, if unrelated activities begin to predominate, then tax-free status is in danger. Obtaining fifty percent (50%) or more of revenues from unrelated activities would be a sure sign of trouble. However, exempt status has been retained even when unrelated income constituted as much as thirty-nine percent (39%) of total revenues—although organizations should not rely on this percentage since all the circumstances have to be considered, not just a mechanical percentage. If unrelated business income exceeds five percent (5%) of total revenues, obtaining professional advice would probably be a good idea.

As mentioned above, there is a mathematical test for one type of organization—a social club exempt under section 501(c)(7). Such a club generally will not have "excessive" unrelated income if receipts from the general public (as opposed to members and their guests) is not over fifteen percent (15%) of gross receipts. In addition, receipts from the general public plus investment income should not exceed thirty-five percent (35%) of gross receipts. The term "gross receipts" includes dues but not unusual items of income such as a one-time sale of club real estate. If the club exceeds these guidelines, its exempt status could be lost, depending on the circumstances. Note that the fifteen–thirty-five percent (15%–35%) tests don't provide any safety for activities which are not traditionally carried on by clubs. Food, entertainment and recreation are types of traditional club activities, but sales of cars or furniture probably would not be considered traditional.

(d)   *Giving Benefits to Private Persons*

A general requirement for most exempt organizations is that no funds be used for the benefit of any private shareholder or individual. This does not mean that reasonable salaries cannot be paid, that reasonable expenses cannot be reimbursed, or that fair value cannot be paid for goods and services. The prohibited private benefit occurs where the organization gives up something without getting an equivalent value in return—excepting, of course, the performance of an exempt function such as scholarship grants or charitable relief. The IRS will especially scrutinize payments to officers, founders, substantial contributors and other related parties. While dealings with such parties are sometimes permitted (however, *see* Part II(Q)(2)), the organization should be prepared to prove that the transactions reflect fair value. Particular problem areas are significant salaries paid to figurehead officers or directors; providing free goods and services to related parties; management fees; loans made without collateral and a fair rate of interest; and property purchases and rental arrangements with insiders. Even salaries to full-time officers should be limited to a reasonable amount based on salaries paid to comparable employees of similar organizations. The organization should also avoid paying compensation as a percentage of net profits unless professional advice is obtained first.

(e)   *Political Activities*

Organizations must also be extremely cautious when engaging in any type of political activity. This includes grants made by the organization to another entity which uses the funds in a political activity.

A section 501(c)(3) organization should not participate in an election campaign or contribute to or endorse any candidate. Voting records of elected officials may be published, but unless done in a nonpartisan manner, there is a potential for trouble.

Section 501(c)(3) organizations have a little more freedom in lobbying to influence legislation. Some of these organizations may elect to spend a certain amount on lobbying by filing IRS Form 5768, but substantial penalties and possible loss of exempt status are imposed if the organization exceeds the permissible amount. Lobbying expenditures for organizations filing Form 5768 are limited to:

> ▸ twenty percent (20%) of the first $500,000.00 spent in performing an exempt function

> ▸ fifteen percent (15%) of the second $500,000.00

> ▸ ten percent (10%) of the third $500,000.00

> ▸ five percent (5%) of any excess

All related organizations are lumped together for the purpose of applying these percentages. Furthermore, total lobbying expenditures cannot exceed $1,000,000.00 per year. Finally, only one-fourth of the above limits may be used for "grassroots" lobbying as distinguished from "direct" lobbying. "Grassroots" lobbying is an attempt to influence the general public, or a segment thereof, with regard to legislation. "Direct" lobbying is where the organization directly contacts government officials to influence legislation.

Note that churches and private foundations are <u>not</u> eligible to make this Form 5768 lobbying election. These entities, together with any other 501(c)(3) organizations which for some reason choose not to make the Form 5768 election, are subject to a different subjective standard with regard to lobbying expenditures. Such an organization may not devote a "substantial" part of its activities to lobbying. Just what is "substantial" depends on all the facts and circumstances, but in one situation five percent (5%) was determined to be "substantial." In any event, the amount of lobbying permitted under the subjective "substantial" test is probably less than that allowed under the special election. Private foundations should also be aware of possible penalty taxes on politically-oriented expenditures (Part II(Q)(2)).

A section 501(c)(4) or (c)(6) organization has more flexibility in political activities than a 501(c)(3) one. Such organizations may engage in lobbying so long as exempt activities, not political ones, remain the primary purpose of the organization. A 501(c)(4) or (c)(6) organization may also participate in election campaigns without losing its exemption, again, provided that exempt activities continue to be the primary purpose. However, Form 1120-POL must be filed if campaign expenditures exceed $100.00, and the organization may become taxable on its net investment income. Thus, campaigning should be undertaken with caution.

(f) Discrimination

Exempt status may also be revoked for various types of discrimination. Racial discrimination causes the most problems, and if the organization's charter or any written policy statement contains such a provision, exempt status is almost certain to be revoked. Religious discrimination causes similar problems; however, a social club exempt under section 501(c)(7) may limit its membership to those belonging to one particular religion. Extreme care should be taken in the drafting of any such restriction. The area of sexual and gender-preference discrimination is somewhat unsettled and a clear answer cannot be given. Of course, an organization wishing to be perfectly safe from challenge should avoid every kind of discrimination.

C. PAYROLL TAXES

(1) Applicability of Payroll Taxes
    (a)   General Provisions
    (b)   Churches and Religious Organizations

(2) Computing Payroll Taxes
    (a)   Income Tax Withholding
    (b)   Social Security (FICA) Taxes
    (c)   Unemployment Taxes

(3) Paying Payroll Taxes
    (a)   Income Taxes Withheld and FICA Taxes
    (b)   Unemployment Taxes

(4) Payroll Tax Returns and Reporting
    (a)   Income Taxes Withheld and FICA Taxes
    (b)   Unemployment Taxes

C. Payroll Taxes

Introductory Note: Since payroll tax rules change from time to time, the information in this chapter can be updated by consulting the *Employer's Tax Guide*, which may be obtained free from any IRS office. This and other information may also be found on the Internet at: www.irs.gov.

(1) Applicability of Payroll Taxes

(a) *General Provisions*

If your nonprofit organization is other than a church or religious order, income taxes must be withheld from employee wages in the same manner that a regular business does. Social Security taxes (also known as Federal Insurance Contribution Act or FICA taxes) must also be withheld and matched by the employer except for employees paid less than $100.00 per year. Federal Unemployment Tax Act (FUTA) taxes are also owed on employees paid $50.00 or more during a calendar quarter unless your organization is tax exempt under section 501(c)(3) of the Internal Revenue Code, in which case no FUTA taxes are owed at all. That section includes most religious, charitable and educational organizations. A nonprofit organization may also be liable for state unemployment taxes; contact an attorney, CPA, or the state unemployment office if you do not know the requirements for your state.

(b) *Churches and Religious Organizations*

Treasurers of churches and religious orders should be aware of the following special rules:

> ▸ Clergy are not treated as employees with respect to their religious work. Instead they are treated as self-employed persons and pay the self-employment tax. There is no FICA or income tax withholding on their salaries. Nor does the church pay any FICA or FUTA taxes on a minister's compensation. Furthermore, clergy members with a conscientious objection to public insurance programs may apply for exemption from the self-employment tax on IRS Form 4361. Applying for this exemption is the responsibility of the individual minister and not the treasurer.

> ▸ Members of a religious order (such as a monastery) are not subject to federal payroll taxes and withholding on work performed for the

order (as distinguished from work performed for outside businesses) unless the entire order elects Social Security coverage. The order is likewise exempt from FUTA taxes.

▸ Church employees other than clergy are subject to income tax withholding. FICA withholding also applies unless the church made a timely election on IRS Form 8274 to treat employees as self-employed persons for FICA purposes. In the case of a new church, this election must be made before the first Form 941 is due for wage payments. In the case of an already existing church, the election must have been made during 1984 or else it is too late to elect out of FICA withholding. In any event, FUTA taxes do not apply to church employees.

(2)   Computing Payroll Taxes

(a)   *Income Tax Withholding*

To determine the correct amount of federal income tax to be withheld from an employee's paycheck, you need the current withholding tables contained in the *Employer's Tax Guide* published by the IRS.

First, select the correct table for that employee. This is based on whether the employee is married or single, and the length of the pay period (weekly, monthly, *etc.*). Next, go down the left-hand column until reaching the amount of the employee's earnings for that pay period. Finally, read across on that row until reaching the column for the number of exemptions on that person's Form W-4 (the IRS form signed by each employee which shows the number of exemptions claimed for withholding purposes). The number you arrive at is the amount to be withheld for federal income taxes from that paycheck.

Where state income taxes apply, a state withholding table should also be obtained. Most such tables are read in the same manner as the federal tables.

(b)   *Social Security (FICA) Taxes*

The amount of FICA tax to be withheld from each paycheck is determined by multiplying two percentage rates times the total earnings. For 2003 and beyond, until changed by Congress, the total of these two rates is 7.65 percent. This consists of 6.2 percent for pure Social Security plus 1.45 percent for Medicare. On federal forms these two rates are applied separately instead of simply using the single percentage of 7.65 percent. This seems confusing but unfortunately that's the way it is.

The employer must pay an additional matching tax equal to the FICA tax withheld from employees.

Only earnings up to a certain amount for each employee are subject to the 6.2 percent pure Social Security tax—and once cumulative annual earnings of an individual exceed this amount, no further 6.2 percent withholding is made for that employee during the rest of the year. This limitation amount increases every year and can be obtained from the IRS. However, it is safe to say that it will always be more than $80,000.00, so if no employees earn more than this annually, the treasurer need not worry about the limitation.

(c) Unemployment Taxes

Unemployment taxes are not withheld from employee wages. Rather, they are a tax imposed on the organization directly.

The federal unemployment (FUTA) tax, if it applies to your organization, is determined by multiplying each employee's wages (up to a certain annual amount) by a percentage rate. (In 2003 the rate was 6.2 percent and the earnings limitation was $7,000.00 per employee.) A partial credit is available against this tax for state unemployment taxes paid. The most current tax rates and earnings limitations can be obtained from the IRS or from Form 940.

FUTA taxes are not owed with respect to employees paid less than $50.00 in a calendar quarter.

State unemployment taxes, if they apply to your organization, are also based on a percentage set by the state multiplied by the employee's earnings up to a certain amount.

(3)   Paying Payroll Taxes

(a) Income Taxes Withheld and FICA Taxes

The federal income and FICA taxes withheld from paychecks, together with the employer's matching share of FICA tax, are combined for purposes of payment to the IRS. Except in two situations (discussed below), these taxes are not paid to the IRS directly, but are deposited with the association's bank together with an IRS Form 8109 coupon. The bank then forwards the funds to the IRS.

The IRS provides a supply of preprinted Form 8109 coupons to the organization. However, it is no excuse for late payment if the organization loses or does not receive these forms. Instead, the organization should contact the IRS or its bank ahead of time for a blank Form 8109-B which you can then fill out to accompany the deposit with the bank.

If the organization is new and has not yet received its Employer Identification Number (Part II(B)(1)(a)), it can send its payment directly to the IRS by the due date, together with an explanation of the situation, instead of making a bank deposit.

If the organization has less than $2,500.00 in total federal income tax withheld and FICA taxes due for the calendar quarter, it can send a check directly to the IRS together with its Form 941 (*see* below).

In all other circumstances, deposits must be made with the bank. For many treasurers (unless the total taxes for the quarter are less than $2,500.00), the easiest way to handle tax deposits is to make them every payday, or within three business days afterwards.

This three-business-day grace period is reduced to one business day if the accumulated undeposited taxes reach $100,000.00.

A monthly deposit schedule is also available, but qualifying for it is complicated and the *Employer's Tax Guide* should be consulted for requirements.

Failure to make timely deposits will result in penalties and interest, even if only one day late, and which increase in percentage and amount as the tardiness grows longer. The penalty (but not the interest) may be waived by the IRS if the organization can prove a "reasonable cause" for the delay. Generally this is limited to disasters such as fire, or death or hospitalization of the treasurer. Excuses such as mere forgetting, confusion within the office, press of business or lack of funds will not be accepted by the IRS.

Furthermore, if the organization fails to pay its withheld taxes, the treasurer and other responsible officials in the organization can have those taxes assessed against them personally. This is an added incentive for the treasurer to see that deposits are made on time. If the organization is short of funds, the treasurer should resist suggestions that other bills be paid first and that the taxes "can be taken care of later"—unless he wants to risk eventually paying those taxes himself. Should the organization get in a situation where it could fall seriously behind on its tax payments, the treasurer should get advice from an attorney or CPA immediately.

The payment due dates for state income taxes withheld vary among states. As with the federal taxes, the treasurer is often personally liable if they are not paid.

(b) *Unemployment Taxes*

Federal unemployment (FUTA) taxes are handled separately for purposes of payment to the IRS.

If the total tax owed for the year is $100.00 or less, it may simply be paid with Form 940 by January 31st of the following year. Often this will be the case where the organization has only a small payroll (and, of course, if it is tax-exempt under section 501(c)(3), there is no FUTA tax at all).

However, if at the end of any calendar quarter the cumulative unpaid FUTA tax is more than $100.00, it must be deposited with the bank, accompanied by a Form 8109 coupon, by the last day of the month after the quarter.

State unemployment funds have their own payment rules—usually any tax due has to be paid quarterly with the state unemployment tax return.

(4) Payroll Tax Returns and Reporting

(a) *Income Taxes Withheld and FICA Taxes*

Just as these federal taxes are combined for deposit purposes, they are also combined for reporting on the payroll tax return, which is IRS Form 941 (*Employer's Quarterly Federal Tax Return*). This is due by the last day of the month after each calendar quarter. Normally the IRS mails out these forms to the organization about a month before the due date, but not receiving these forms is not an excuse for late filing.

It contains a summary of total wages paid, total income tax withheld, total FICA taxes due (employer's and employees' shares), and a breakdown of when those amounts arose during the quarter. The treasurer should be sure that the amount of tax deposits is shown correctly on Form 941. Showing more deposits than were actually made will result in a substantial penalty.

States with an income tax provide their own forms for reporting withheld state taxes.

For each employee, a statement of annual earnings and taxes must be provided on Form W-2 as described at Chapter 8(G).

(b) *Unemployment Taxes*

The federal unemployment (FUTA) tax return is Form 940, which is filed annually by January 31st after the end of the year. If a state unemployment tax applies, a state form should also be filed, which is usually done on a quarterly basis.

D. CHECKLIST OF REPORTS
AND PAYMENTS

D.   Checklist of Reports and Payments

Almost all but the smallest associations must file reports with federal and state government agencies in order to maintain their tax-exempt status. Those with employees must make payments of withheld wage, Social Security (FICA) and unemployment compensation taxes, and must file reports on the payments made. Some of these reports and payments must be made monthly, some quarterly and some annually. Unless another officer has been designated to see that all this is done, the treasurer should assume the responsibility. Very few people are familiar with all these procedures, and a new treasurer, especially, can find them confusing. Frequently volunteer treasurers neglect them either through ignorance or because they are not willing to take the necessary trouble. However, failure to make these payments and file the required reports can lead to serious trouble for the organization.

The best way to avoid any neglect of reports and payments when due is for the treasurer to set up a reminder checklist of all reports and payments for which the association is responsible. If the association has not used a checklist earlier, the conscientious treasurer should prepare one at the start of his term. He should add to it when necessary, and he should explain its use to his successor.

The checklist can remind the treasurer of exactly what filings and payments are required, the due dates, what forms to use, and where to obtain the information to be reported. The office staff can use the checklist to prepare the appropriate reports and checks for the treasurer's signature, and thus save him time. When the treasurer is absent, the office staff can use the checklist to prepare reports to be signed by another officer. The attached illustration shows one form that a checklist might take. It includes full information on federal government requirements only because the reports and payments due under state law vary from one state to another. An association should consult a specialist, if necessary, to find out what state requirements it must fulfill and add them to the checklist. These may include payment of state (and sometimes city) withholding taxes, reporting of wages paid, payment of state unemployment compensation taxes, payment of annual corporation fees to the Secretary of State, and perhaps other items.

Other non-governmental due dates for items such as wage payments, insurance premiums and rental expense can be added to the checklist as needed by the organization.

TREASURER'S CHECKLIST OF FILINGS AND PAYMENTS

FEDERAL

ACTION	TO	FORM	FREQUENCY, DUE DATE
Deposit Federal Withholding Taxes	Bank	IRS Form 8109	Every payday, or see Part II(C)(3)(a)
File Federal Employer's Tax Return	IRS	IRS Form 941	Quarterly, by End of Following Month
Distribute IRS Form W-2	All Employees	W-2, Wage and Tax Statement	Annually, by January 31
File Form W-2	Social Security Administration	Same	Annually, by February 28
Distribute IRS Form 1099-MISC	Nonemployees Paid $600.00 or More	1099-MISC, Miscellaneous Compensation	Annually, by January 31
File Form 1099-MISC	IRS	Same	Annually, by February 28
File Federal Unemployment Return	IRS	IRS Form 940	Annually, by January 31
File Federal Tax Return	IRS	IRS Form 990 or 990-PF	Annually, by 15th day of Fifth Month After Year-end

STATE
[Variable, According to State Law]

Pay State Withholding Taxes			
File State Report of Wages Paid			
Pay State Unemployment Tax			
File State Unemployment Tax Return			

File State Annual Corporate Report	Secretary of State	Annual

File State Sales Tax Return		

OTHER
(Will Depend on Particular Organization)

Pay Employees		Semi-monthly (Example, May Vary)

Fill out Record of Wages Withheld	Keep on File	When Paid

Make Rental Payment	Landlord	Monthly

Pay Hospitalization Insurance Premium	Insurance Company	

Pay Property Insurance Premium	Insurance Company	

Remit Dues to National Headquarters		

E. SINGLE OR DOUBLE ENTRY BOOKKEEPING?

(1)   Single Entry Bookkeeping

(2)   Double Entry Bookkeeping

E.   Single or Double Entry Bookkeeping?

All methods of bookkeeping generally fall into two categories: single entry or double entry. The method we have shown in Chapter 4 is an example of single entry bookkeeping. In other words, only a single entry is made into the books for each transaction.

Double entry bookkeeping, on the other hand, is the method used by professional accountants. Here, each transaction generates two entries at the same time. For instance, when a member pays dues, an entry is made in the cash account to show the increase in cash, while another entry is made in the dues income account to show this additional revenue. Or if a check is written for postage, one entry is made to reduce the cash account accordingly and another is made to postage expense to show this additional cost.

Accountants call one of these entries a "debit" and the other a "credit." For each transaction, debits will always equal credits. Likewise, the total debits and credits in the entire accounting system will always be equal.

We considered including a chapter in this book on how to perform double entry accounting, but finally decided against it. To properly explain the basics of double entry accounting would require well over a hundred pages; generally a full-length book is used to instruct students. Formal high school and college courses are devoted to just the essentials.

For this reason we felt that a new volunteer treasurer—who had no accounting training—would not be willing to invest the extensive time needed to learn the double entry method—nor would it be reasonable for the association to expect him to do so. And in situations where the treasurer already has an accounting background, a "how to" chapter on the double entry method would simply be repetitious.

If a new treasurer does wish to learn double entry bookkeeping, there are many excellent instructional books available at the public library, and such courses are offered in most adult education and college programs.

Our focus here will be on whether an association should use one accounting method or the other.

(1)   Single Entry Bookkeeping

As indicated above, for the new treasurer with no accounting background, the single entry system, such as described in Chapter 4, is the easiest method to use and understand. Even where the current treasurer understands double entry accounting, the association must consider that future treasurers may not be so trained, and thus they may be unable to perform the job if the association is on a double entry system.

Of course, if the treasurer is assisted by a trained accountant, the treasurer's own lack of a double entry education is not so critical, and the association need not be restricted to the single entry system.

(2)   Double Entry Bookkeeping

The double entry method should be considered whenever the association has present and future treasurers with the necessary background or has the services of other persons trained in accounting. The double entry method is the "universal language" of professional accountants and may actually be easier for such persons to understand than the single entry method. The double entry method is also more compatible with computer usage.

Another advantage is the "self-balancing" aspect of the system. Since debits should always equal credits, any discrepancy between total debits and credits indicates that an error has been made (Part II(H)). The same kind of error in single entry records is not so readily detected since the system has no internal check against itself.

Finally, the double entry method is most suitable where the association has a large volume of transactions. If there are just a few transactions, the treasurer can practically "see everything at once" and it is relatively easy to arrive at the proper account balances. On the other hand, where the number of transactions during a month exceeds the treasurer's capacity to remember or to see on a few sheets, then arriving at proper account balances is easier under the double entry method since all affected accounts are continuously updated after each transaction. For instance, in our previous example, when the receipt of dues is recorded under the double entry method, both the cash account and the dues income account are adjusted at the same time.

F. CASH OR ACCRUAL METHOD?

F.   Cash or Accrual Method?

A new organization must choose whether to use the cash basis or the accrual method of accounting. The cash basis means that income, such as dues payments or literature sales, is received only as the cash (or check) is received, and expenses are recorded only when a check is written for payment. The cash basis accounting system relies heavily on the checkbook. The accrual method, on the other hand, recognizes income when earned, which is prior to the receipt of cash where credit is involved. Expenses are recorded when incurred, which may be before payment is actually made.

The cash method, being based on the checkbook, is generally simpler than the accrual method and is used most often by smaller organizations. On the other hand, the accrual method is more professional and accurate since receivables and payables should be considered in addition to cash receipts and disbursements.

To illustrate this principle with an example, suppose that an association which sponsored a seminar has collected cash of $1,000.00 and is owed an additional $100.00 by participants who have not yet paid as of the end of the year. Cash payments for expenses are $300.00, but the speaker's fee expense of $600.00 is still unpaid at year-end. A cash basis statement shows a profit of $700.00 ($1,000.00–$300.00), but an accrual basis statement shows a profit of $200.00 ($1,100.00–$900.00). The accrual basis statement is more accurate since the cash basis statement has not reflected the $600.00 speaker's fee and the $100.00 due from participants.

As this example shows, the cash basis method is more prone to manipulation than the accrual method. An association officer whose term is expiring could make a cash basis organization appear to be in great financial shape by simply not paying bills near the end of his term. The association and successor officers, however, are ill-served by this form of deception.

Which method should your organization use? The cash method is fine for a small organization where the unpaid bills and receivables, if any, are relatively minor. However, as will be shown below, the accrual method needn't be much more difficult. If the organization gets larger, a change to accrual may be necessary anyway. And this switch is easier for the treasurer and less confusing to financial statement readers when the organization is small.

The primary objection to the accrual method is complexity. If an organization followed the "perpetual" approach to the accrual method, this complaint would be well-founded. Under the perpetual approach, the accrual method is used throughout the year for each transaction. For instance, an entry is made to record the sale of association literature on credit at the time the sale is made, and then another entry is made later when the cash is received to show the collection of the accounts receivable. This technique, of course, requires twice as many entries as the cash basis method, under which the sale is recorded only at the time of payment and no accounts receivable are ever shown.

The "periodic" version of the accrual method is much easier. Here the accounting records are kept on the cash basis all year long, but an adjustment is made to the accrual method at year-end. The adjustment consists of adding up all amounts due the association on the last day of the year and using this amount to increase income and create accounts receivable. Likewise, all expense bills unpaid as of year-end are added up and used to increase expenses and create accounts payable. To complete the process, the corresponding cash-to-accrual adjustment on the prior year's books is reversed. This reversal is necessary because otherwise these items of income and expense would be double-counted—once on last year's books because of the adjustment made in that year, and once on this year's books as the cash was actually paid or received. By reversing last year's accruals in the current year, this double-counting is avoided.

In short, the periodic version of the accrual method provides all the simplicity of the cash basis for day-to-day operations during the year. Yet the accuracy of the accrual method is preserved for year-end statements merely by making the simple adjustments mentioned above.

Suppose an organization using the periodic version wants to present monthly or quarterly financial statements in addition to the year-end ones. Since day-to-day operations are on the cash basis, an adjustment of the type mentioned above must be made at the end of each monthly or quarterly period if such statements are desired on an accrual basis.

Let's illustrate the periodic principle with another seminar example:

<u>FACTS</u>:

Seminar income due and unpaid at end of prior year	$ 500
Seminar income due and unpaid at end of this year	700
Cash received during year for seminars (including	
payments for seminars held in the prior year)	8,000
Unpaid seminar expenses at end of prior year	300
Unpaid seminar expenses at end of this year	400
Cash paid out during year for seminar expenses	
(including payments on expenses incurred in	
the prior year)	7,000

Based on these facts, the cash basis statement would be as follows:

<u>CASH BASIS STATEMENT</u>:

Seminar income	8,000
Seminar expenses	(7,000)
Seminar profit	$1,000

To convert to an accrual basis statement, the following adjustments would be made:

PERIODIC ADJUSTMENTS TO THE ACCRUAL BASIS:

SEMINAR INCOME:

Cash received during year	$8,000
Plus seminar income due and unpaid at end of this year	700
Minus seminar income due and unpaid at end of prior year	(500)
Accrual basis seminar income during year	$8,200

SEMINAR EXPENSES:

Cash paid out for seminar expenses	$7,000
Plus unpaid expenses at end of this year	400
Minus unpaid expenses at end of prior year	(300)
Accrual basis seminar expenses during year	$7,100

After making the above adjustments, the accrual basis statement would appear as follows:

ACCRUAL BASIS STATEMENT:

Seminar income	$8,200
Seminar expenses	(7,100)
Seminar profit	$1,100

In addition, the balance sheet at year-end would show accounts receivable of $700.00 and accounts payable of $400.00.

What happens if income which is due at the end of the year later becomes uncollectable? For accrual basis organizations, if the uncollectability could be foreseen before the financial statements for that year are prepared, the uncollectable amount should be subtracted from income due at the end of that year.

If the uncollectability is not discovered until later in the next year, then the proper procedure is to do nothing other than follow the steps in the illustration above. The original full amount of income due at the end of the prior year is still reversed in the next year, but since the full amount of cash was not received, the accrual basis income for the next year will automatically be reduced to the appropriate level to reflect the loss if the adjustments are made as shown in the above illustration.

If a cash basis organization cannot collect income that is due, no adjustment is necessary since such organizations only show the cash actually received as their income.

G. BLOCKING FRAUDS AND THEFT

(1)   Payroll Frauds

(2)   Preventing Theft of Other Assets

(3)   The "Lost Check" Swindle

(4)   Protecting the Checkbook

G.   Blocking Frauds and Theft

(1)   Payroll Frauds

One type of fraud encountered in large organizations but seldom in small ones is the padded payroll. Here an employee who dies or leaves the organization is still kept on the payroll, and the embezzler then cashes the extra paycheck for himself. In a small organization, of course, everyone should know who is really working and who isn't. In a large organization this type of fraud can be detected by periodically comparing the payroll records to the actual employees—which can be easily handled in connection with annual salary reviews or other employee evaluations.

Alternatively, payroll records can be compared to independent documentary evidence of employment such as time cards or production reports. Another technique used by auditors is to compare the signed endorsements on payroll checks to the signatures on employee W-4 forms (the IRS form filled out by an employee showing the number of exemptions claimed for wage withholding purposes).

(2)   Preventing Theft of Other Assets

Another problem is the pilfering of goods such as stationery, supplies or items for sale. This problem can be minimized in a number of ways.

First, if the asset records and the actual assets themselves are handled by different individuals, a theft may be discovered when the assets are counted and compared to the records. This is because normally only legitimate withdrawals are shown on the records, and thus the recorded amount of assets would exceed the actual amount on hand if there was a theft. Such a counting and comparison process should be performed at least annually—a normal procedure for any commercial business, which is called "taking an inventory."

The frequency of taking inventories depends on the nature of the assets involved. To use an extreme example, a nonprofit clinic might count its narcotics at the end of every day, other prescription drugs monthly, cough syrup annually, and tongue depressors never.

If the custodian of the assets does have access to the asset records or is able to deceive the record keeper, then the counting and comparison process will not uncover the shortage since the records and assets will agree. In this situation the best way to detect a significant shortage is by budget analysis. The inventory shortage will be reflected in the financial report as increased usage, and should the total usage of goods significantly exceed the budget amount (or be out of the proper proportion to sales or another account), then an investigation should be made.

Needless to say, the custodian of the assets should make sure they are appropriately guarded. We are concerned not only about theft by the custodian, but by others as well. Again, the protection effort should be proportioned to the value of the assets. Extremely high value items (negotiable securities, gems, precious coins) should be kept in a bank safe deposit box or at least an office safe. Other items which are "worth stealing" can be kept in locked rooms or cabinets when unattended. Pencils, paper clips and other minor items probably should not be locked up as the inconvenience may outweigh the value of protection. However, if experience shows that pilferage of these items is a problem, then they may have to be locked up, too.

Larger associations, in particular, should also take steps to prevent strangers from roaming at will through the office. For instance, a thief may pose as a repairman and walk out with typewriters and other equipment. Or the thief may use the visit as an opportunity to "case" the office for a future theft. Such persons may claim to be salesmen, charitable collectors, or friends of employees. To prevent this problem, the credentials of unknown visitors should be verified (not just glanced at), such as by close examination of identifying documents, telephone confirmation with the visitor's company, or approval by someone in the association. Once inside the office, the person should be escorted by an association employee. A "sign-in" book at the front desk is helpful, but should not be relied on by itself—it's unlikely a thief would write down his true name.

(3)   The "Lost Check" Swindle

This type of fraud occurs when someone to whom you have written a check later claims falsely that it was "lost" and requests a replacement check. The unsuspecting treasurer will stop payment on the old check and write a new one. Then the person will cash both the old and the new checks at different locations, usually retail or grocery stores. Under banking laws, the association can be liable to pay both checks notwithstanding the stop-payment order. This is because stores cashing checks in their normal course of business, unless they have reason to believe something is amiss, are entitled to have these checks honored. (Of course, if the check really was lost and a third person attempted to cash it, this would be a forgery and the association should not be liable. The problem we are concerned with here is where the named payee cashes both checks made out to him.)

This swindle most commonly occurs with an ex-employee's final paycheck, especially for a "nomadic" type of temporary worker or a person who is leaving town or was disgruntled upon termination. It almost never occurs when the check was written to an established business, to an employee who remains on the payroll, or to a person with roots in the community.

One way to protect yourself against this kind of scam is to have association checks bear the notation "VOID IF CASHED AFTER SIXTY DAYS." Then if a person suspiciously claims that his check was lost, you can make him wait about seventy days or so and then issue a new check if the first one has not been cashed yet (call the bank to confirm this). A later attempt to cash the original check should then be invalid because of the sixty-day notice. Payment should still be stopped on it, however, and the person should pay the bank charge for doing so, especially if the first check had been handed to him personally and it is clearly his fault for losing it.

If association checks do not have this printed sixty-day notation, you can still type or write such a notice by hand on employees' final paychecks or in other situations where the recipient of the check is not already known to be trustworthy.

(4)   Protecting the Checkbook

If the association's checkbook is kept in a building where strangers may enter, precautions should be taken against the theft of blank checks. This is a problem in office buildings where other tenants or the janitorial staff leave doors unlocked when the treasurer is not around. Thieves can pose as cleaning, delivery or sales personnel.

Clever thieves will steal one or more checks from the back or middle of the checkbook, rather than the front, to delay discovery of the theft. In theory, the entity cashing the check, such as a bank, is liable for money lost due to forged signatures on checks. However, even if the association ultimately suffers no financial loss, the treasurer will spend considerable time visiting the bank, filing police reports, and possibly testifying in court. The association's legitimate checks may start bouncing before the loss is detected, leading to further inconvenience and embarrassment.

Several strategies may help reduce these risks:

    (a) Avoid having blank checks presigned. These are easier for thieves to cash, and unlike the situation where signatures are forged, the association may wind up suffering the loss.

    (b) Keep the checkbook at home or locked up.

(c) Don't have the association's name and/or the names of author-ized signers printed on the checks or kept near the checkbook. This makes it harder for a thief to know what name to sign on the checks. In particular, keep canceled checks and the signature card away from the checkbook so the thief does not have a sample sig-nature to copy.

(d) Reconcile the bank statement monthly (Chapter 4(G)), which should reveal any stolen checks which have been cashed so that these can be reported to police and the bank.

(e) If there is evidence of a break-in or other suspicious circum-stances, go through the remaining checks to determine that all check numbers are present and accounted for. As mentioned above, thieves may steal from the back or middle of the check-book.

H. FINDING ERRORS

H.   Finding Errors

Sometimes a treasurer finds that two sets of figures which should add up to the same total instead show a difference. There are a few shortcuts that sometimes help locate the difference. For instance, in double entry bookkeeping, if the difference is due to omitting either a debit or a credit amount from an entry (in other words, making a one-sided entry), the difference can be found by simply scanning the records for the amount in question and then seeing whether both a debit and a credit have been recorded.

If the difference is due to reversing the side of an entry (having two debits or two credits instead of one debit and one credit), the error can be located by dividing the difference in half and then scanning the records for such an amount and ascertaining whether debits and credits have been correctly presented. Obviously the difference must be an even number—not an odd number—in order to be caused by a reversing error alone.

If the error is due to a transposed digit such as 51 written as 15, or 291 as 219, then the difference will always be divisible by nine. Thus, the difference between 51 and 15 is 36, which divides evenly by 9. Similarly, the difference between 291 and 219 is 72, also divisible by 9. Therefore if the difference divides evenly by 9, look for a transposed digit. Furthermore, you can get some idea of the particular digits to look for because the number which results when the difference is divided by nine happens to be, in turn, the difference between the transposed digits. For instance, the difference between 91 and 19 is 72, which, divided by 9 is 8. Eight represents the difference between the digits of 9 and 1. You would then scan the tens and ones columns for 91 or 19, investigating each such number found for possible error. Similarly, the difference between 51 and 15 is 36, which divided by 9 yields 4—the difference between the digits 5 and 1. However, it is also the difference between 6 and 2, 7 and 3, 8 and 4, and 9 and 5. Thus the tens and ones columns would be scanned for the digits 04, 40, 15, 51, 26, 62, 37, 73, 48, 84, 59 and 95. This sounds complicated but really isn't. Just look for two digits with a difference of 4.

So far we have looked at transposed digits in the tens and ones columns. Transposed digits in other columns are found just as easily, and the columns can be pinpointed by counting the number of digits in the difference. Thus, if the transposition was 15,000 and 51,000, the difference is 36,000. Divided by 9 is 4,000. Since the 36 occurs before 3 zeros (36,000), the transposed digits (different from each other by 4) are found in the fourth and fifth columns (thousands and ten thousands). These two columns would then be scanned for digits with a difference between them of 4.

For further information on finding errors in bank statement reconciliations, see Chapter 4(G)(1).

I. PREPARING THE ANNUAL FINANCIAL REPORT

(1)   General Guidelines

(2)   Balance Sheet (Statement of Financial Position)

(3)   Income Statement (Statement of Activities)

(4)   Footnote Disclosures

(5)   Using a CPA's Services
      (a)   The Audit
      (b)   The Compilation
      (c)   The Review

I.   Preparing the Annual Financial Report

(1)   General Guidelines

The financial report is the end product of the treasurer's work. Its purpose is to explain the association's financial condition to officers, directors and members—and in certain circumstances, to donors, bankers, parent associations, grant-making organizations or the government.

The two most important financial statements in the report are the balance sheet or "statement of financial position" (showing assets and liabilities) and the income statement or "statement of activities" (showing profit or loss). In addition, there may also be other specialized financial statements such as a "statement of cash flows", depending on the circumstances.

There is no fixed format which must be followed (unless dictated by some regulation applicable to your association)—the best format will depend on the particular association and the needs of its financial statement users. A few general guidelines should be followed. For instance, the name of the organization, the title of the statement and the time period covered should be at the top of each statement.

The most important principle is to fully and meaningfully inform financial statement readers. All financial information that readers might consider important must be disclosed either in the body of the statements or in footnotes. On the other hand, the statements should not be cluttered with obviously insignificant information. Remember that most readers have only a limited amount of time and attention to devote to the statements.

The treasurer's careful judgment is required to determine the level of detail presented. For instance, combining rent, salaries, insurance and stationery into the single category of "office expense" usually would be too vague to assist financial statement users. On the other hand, most of us have seen lengthy reports consisting of a mass of individual transactions which may be just as difficult to understand as an over-simplified statement. If highly-detailed reports must be presented because of some regulation or bylaw, consider presenting more concise statements as a supplement, allowing readers to choose which set of statements they wish to review.

While day-to-day accounting records must be kept in exact cents, all amounts shown on the report can be rounded off to the nearest dollar instead of showing pennies.

Consistency in presentation is usually desirable so that prior years' statements can be compared to the current year. Thus, if utilities are included in rent expense one year but are shown separately in another year, both accounts will be hard for readers to evaluate on a comparative basis.

On the other hand, changes may be necessary to make the statements more meaningful. If several large costs of differing natures have been previously lumped into "office expense" as discussed above, the treasurer probably should expand the presentation. In this situation the change should be disclosed in the statements, and a supplemental schedule showing the breakdown of "office expense" for one or more prior years might also be considered. Of course, a change in the handling of extremely minor items need not be disclosed.

(2)   Balance Sheet

The balance sheet (also called the Statement of Financial Position) is a financial snapshot of the assets and liabilities at year-end. As discussed in Part II(P), the fund balance is simply the difference between the association's assets and liabilities. It is also called "net assets", or using business terminology, it is the association's "net worth."

The balance sheet may be shown with two sides: assets on the left, and liabilities and fund balance on the right. Alternatively, the balance sheet may have a single column divided into upper and lower segments—upper for assets, and lower for liabilities and fund balance. In either case, the total of all assets will always equal the combined total of all liabilities and the fund balance.

The asset section itself is usually divided into two categories. The first category is for "current" assets—that is, cash and bank balances (usually shown at the top), accounts receivable, inventories and other items which are expected to be turned into cash or consumed within one year. The second category is for "long-term" assets—usually buildings, equipment and long-term investments (those that are not expected to be sold within one year). Investments, such as stocks and bonds, are shown at their market value as of the statement date. For instance, if the balance sheet is for December 31, the newspaper for January 1st of the next year would be consulted to find the December 31 stock values. Any change in market values since the previous statement (or the date of purchase, if it happened during the year) is shown as an income or loss item on the income statement.

The liability section is handled similarly. "Current" liabilities (typically, unpaid bills) are for debts to be paid within one year. "Long-term" liabilities are all others. For installment debts, the cumulative principal payments over the next twelve months are generally shown in current liabilities, while the rest of the loan balance would remain in long-term liabilities.

A sample balance sheet (or Statement of Financial Position) is shown here:

ABC ASSOCIATION

BALANCE SHEET

DECEMBER 31, 20XX

<u>ASSETS</u>		<u>LIABILITIES</u>	
Current Assets:		Current Liabilities:	
Cash in bank	$1,000	Accounts Payable	$ 800
Accounts Receivable	500	Current portions of	
Inventory for resale	<u>2,000</u>	long-term debt	<u>1,000</u>
Total current	<u>3,500</u>	Total current	<u>1,800</u>
Long-term Assets:		Long-term Liabilities:	
Office equipment	4,000	Auto loan	700
Automobile	3,000	Building loan	39,000
Building	50,000	($40,000 total)	
Less depreciation	(10,000)	Total long-term	<u>39,700</u>
Total long-term	<u>47,000</u>		
		Total Liabilities	$41,500
		Fund Balance	$ 9,000
		TOTAL LIABILITIES &	
TOTAL ASSETS	<u>$50,500</u>	FUND BALANCE	<u>$50,500</u>

(3)   Income Statement

The income statement (also called the Statement of Activities) reflects the association's financial performance over a period of time, such as one month or one year. Income items are shown at the top, followed by expense items. The difference between income and expenses is the "change in fund balance," or "change in net assets," or to use business terminology, the net profit or loss.

Income items are sometimes broken down into two categories: Support (consisting of gifts, contributions, and grants), and Revenue (all other kinds of income, such as sales and interest).

Expenses may be shown either by type of payment or by functional purpose of the payment. A type-of-payment listing would show such categories such as salaries, rent, insurance, postage and telephone. If a functional presentation is used, all expenses of whatever nature would be grouped into three broad categories: program services, fundraising, and management and general. "Program services" are activities directly in furtherance of the association's purposes. This category might be further broken down into various subcategories for individual programs. In the case of a professional association these could be member education, legislative lobbying and ethical enforcement.

"Fundraising" expenses are self-explanatory—they are the costs incurred to obtain money such as salaries for solicitors or printing and postage for a mass mailing. The "management and general" category is for everything else—primarily office and overhead expenses.

The functional expense presentation is preferred whenever the organization obtains a substantial amount of donations from the general public. This allows donors to see how much of each dollar contributed goes directly into worthwhile programs as opposed to being spent for fundraising or administrative expenses. If this format is used, the organization should also show a supplemental schedule of expenses classified by type of payment, such as salaries, rent, phone, postage, and so forth. And vice versa, if the organization presents its main income statement in a type-of-payment format, a supplemental schedule should be included showing expenses in functional categories. These supplemental expense schedules can be shown in the footnotes to the financial statements (*see* below).

A sample income statement (or Statement of Activities) is shown here:

ABC ASSOCIATION

INCOME STATEMENT

FOR THE YEAR ENDED DECEMBER 31, 20XX

Support:

Contributions	$2,000	
Government grant	1,500	
Total Support	3,500	

Revenue:

Member dues	5,000	
Literature sales	1,000	
Interest income	200	
Total Revenue	6,200	
Total Support and Revenue		$9,700

Expenses:

Program Services:		
Scholarship Fund	2,000	
Building shelter at park	1,500	
Sponsoring student team	2,000	
Fundraising	500	
Management and General	800	
Total Expenses		6,800
Change in Fund Balance		2,900
Fund Balance at Beginning of Year		6,100
Fund Balance at End of Year		$9,000

If the organization wished to have expenses classified by type of payment rather than by functional purpose, its income statement would appear like this:

ABC ASSOCIATION

INCOME STATEMENT

FOR THE YEAR ENDED DECEMBER 31, 20XX

Support:

Contributions	$2,000	
Government grant	1,500	
Total Support	3,500	

Revenue:

Member dues	5,000	
Literature sales	1,000	
Interest income	200	
Total Revenue	6,200	
Total Support and Revenue		$9,700

Expenses:

Salaries	500	
Rent	1,000	
Printing	300	
Telephone	600	
Travel	1,000	
Building materials	1,200	
Scholarships	2,000	
Depreciation	200	
Total Expenses		6,800
Change in Fund Balance		2,900
Fund Balance at Beginning of Year		6,100
Fund Balance at End of Year		$9,000

(4) Footnote Disclosures

Certain important items of financial information are not contained in the balance sheet or income statement, but still should be disclosed. These items are placed in the footnotes. The footnotes are simply narrative descriptions (usually numbered) which are at the end of the financial report. Common footnotes would cover the following matters:

▸ The tax status of the organization. If it is tax exempt, the Internal Revenue Code section number for the exemption should be cited.

▸ The basic accounting principles followed by the organization. Most important here would be whether it is on the cash or the accrual basis (Part II(F)). Other principles might be the methods of accounting for inventories, bad debts, investment values, or the depreciation of assets. The market value of investments at year-end should be disclosed here if not shown on the balance sheet itself.

▸ The nature and effect of any changes in accounting principles during the year (Part II(L)).

▸ The interest rates and maturity dates of long-term debts, the expiration dates of long-term leases, and key information regarding other commitments such as pension plans, collective bargaining agreements and employment contracts.

▸ The amount of payments that must be made annually over the next five years for existing leases and long-term debts.

▸ Any significant related party transactions. For instance, if the association rents its office space from a board member, the relevant details should be disclosed to avoid any appearance of impropriety.

▸ Any contingent liabilities such as lawsuits threatened or pending, Internal Revenue Service audits in process, or another organization's loans that have been guaranteed by the association.

▸ Any important events (especially adverse ones) that have occurred since year-end. For instance, if the home office was destroyed by fire after year-end, but before the issuance of the financial statements, this should be disclosed.

(5)   Using a CPA's Services

If the association uses the assistance of a certified public accountant in preparing its financial report, you need to understand the differences between the three types of report services that a CPA provides:

(a) *The Audit*

This is the highest level of report that a CPA can render. Here the CPA performs numerous tests of the accounting records on a sample basis and then expresses his professional opinion on the overall reliability of the financial statements. Obviously, this is the most costly option for the association to take. Many small associations do not have an audit unless something in the financial situation is believed to be amiss, or the association is obligated to do so by its own bylaws, or by the requirement of a grantor or parent association. Also, it should be noted that an audit is not an absolute guarantee of the financial statements, is not designed to uncover minor defalcations or errors, and does not ensure the detection of even larger frauds if they are sophisticated enough or the embezzler has enlisted the cooperation of other association employees.

(b)   The Compilation

This is the exact opposite of an audit. The CPA takes the association's year-end account balances and puts them into a neat report format. However, the CPA assumes no responsibility for the accuracy of the figures. No precautions are taken against errors or embezzlement. Of course, a compilation is much less costly than an audit. Compilations can fall into two groups: (i) a regular compilation which is suitable for distribution to banks, other agencies and the public, and (ii) a shorter compilation for internal use only which can be without footnote disclosures of accounting policies, loan and lease terms, and other significant financial matters.

(c)   The Review

Midway between an audit and a compilation is the "review." This is much less extensive than a full audit and the CPA does not attempt to look for problems everywhere. However, the CPA does ask some questions and applies a few elementary tests to uncover obvious mistakes or oversights in certain areas. No professional opinion is given on the financial statements as a whole.

J. HANDLING THE IRS AUDIT

(1)   The Audit Process

(2)   Immunity from Audit

(3)   Cutting Through the Red Tape

(4)   Forms You May Be Asked to Sign

(5)   Principles of Handling an Audit

J.   Handling the IRS Audit

(1)   The Audit Process

Sooner or later almost every organization will undergo some type of IRS audit procedure. The audit may be limited to a single question posed by the IRS which can be answered by mail, or may include either a trip by association representatives to the IRS office or a visit by an IRS field auditor to the association's office. The audit may involve an investigation into tax-exempt status, unrelated business income, payroll taxes, or some combination of the above.

Regardless of what type of audit is encountered, the organization will first deal with an IRS person responsible for initial contact with taxpayers—usually this person is called an "examining agent." After research and investigation, the agent reaches a conclusion on the organization's exempt status and tax liability. The agent's work is then reviewed by a supervisor. When interpretation of the tax law is an issue, the agent may request technical advice from the IRS national office, and in such cases the organization has the opportunity to present its views to the national office for consideration.

If the organization is found to be in full compliance with the tax law, a "no change letter" is usually issued and this ends the matter. However, if the agent concludes that additional tax is owed, a Revenue Agent's Report (RAR) will be issued, and the organization must then decide whether to concede or to appeal within the IRS. Contrary to what some people believe, the RAR is not gospel and the appellate division of the IRS is not just a rubber stamp. The appellate division frequently modifies an RAR to the organization's advantage and occasionally will completely reverse the examining agent's decision. Therefore, unless the dollars in question are extremely small or the issue is clearly "cut and dried," an appeal is often a good idea.

The appeal process consists of a written protest (except in certain small cases) and an informal conference with the appeals officer. The appeal must be requested and the written protest filed within 30 days of the date of the IRS letter confirming the RAR; this is popularly referred to as a "30-day letter." The IRS usually grants an extension of the 30-day period if requested before the end of the 30 days.

Your chances of resolving the case at this level are good since one function of an appeals officer is to negotiate a mutually agreeable settlement. Both the organization and the IRS may make settlement proposals and, depending on the circumstances, the appeals officer may be willing to "horse-trade" or split the difference.

If a settlement cannot be reached at the appeals level, the IRS will issue a "90-day letter," which means that within 90 days the organization must either pay the tax or file a petition in the U.S. Tax Court; no extensions are possible. If the organization pays the tax, the Tax Court cannot be used but a refund suit can be filed in the U.S. District Court or the U.S. Claims Court.

(2)   Immunity from Audit

As a general rule the IRS can audit anyone in any manner it chooses. There are a few limited exceptions:

▸ The statute of limitations on assessing tax is generally three years after the tax return in question was filed. Usually this return is Form 990-T. If you didn't file Form 990-T but fully described all income on Form 990, you are probably still okay. The limitation period can be longer if no return is filed or there is fraud or a significant underreporting of income (more than 25 percent).

▸ Churches can be audited only with the approval of the Regional IRS Commissioner and after the church has received proper written notice 15 days in advance. There are also other restrictions on the scope of IRS audits of churches. The advice of an attorney or CPA may be desirable in this situation.

▸ Once a full audit of a particular year has been completed, the year cannot be reaudited unless the IRS explains in writing why this is necessary.

▸ If the organization has been audited in either of the two years preceding the year in question and the audit resulted in no change to tax liability, the IRS will generally refrain from auditing the year in question unless there are special circumstances. For churches, the period is five years instead of just two years.

If any of these exceptions appear to apply to your organization, immediately point them out to the IRS agent.

(3)   Cutting Through the Red Tape

Occasionally the IRS computer will spew out letter after letter to your organization asking for copies of returns, payment of penalties and so forth. Eventually the letters may become threatening, indicating that the organization's assets will be seized if compliance is not prompt. Never ignore an IRS letter, but respond in writing to the address provided, either giving the IRS what it wants if the request is justified, or stating why the request is unjustified. Always attach a copy of the IRS notice to your reply. If the IRS request is unjustified and correspondence through normal channels has failed to stop the stream of computer notices, contact the IRS Problem Resolution Office which specializes in straightening out such mixups. The Problem Resolution Office is also helpful in tracking down tax payments or other items that seem to have been lost within the IRS computer system.

NOTE: The organization may receive a computer letter claiming that the tax return for a prior year was not filed. If it was filed, send a written reply stating the exact name and federal identification number on the return and the IRS Service Center it was mailed to. Don't send a copy of the return at this time—the IRS may think this duplicate is an original return and could assess penalties for late filing. If, after correspondence, the IRS specifically requests a duplicate, write "DUPLICATE" in large red letters across the first page of the return to prevent a mixup. Include a copy of any proof of filing you have, such as a certified mail receipt. If the situation is not resolved after two rounds of correspondence, contact the Problem Resolution Office.

When communicating with the IRS, several guidelines should be kept in mind. First, do not rely on phone calls to the IRS to solve a problem. A phone call may be useful to arrange a meeting or to determine where letters should be sent—but otherwise phone calls usually seem to be ineffective. Second, never mail original documents or your only copies of documents to the IRS. Send only copies of what you are retaining in your files. (Also, keep copies of all correspondence from and to the IRS.) Third, attach to your letter a copy of the IRS notice you are responding to. This assists the IRS in handling your correspondence. Fourth, sometimes it is helpful to use certified mail. This protects you against the common problem of sending a response to the IRS and then later getting a nasty computer letter stating that you never sent a response.

(4)   Forms You May Be Asked to Sign

The IRS has literally hundreds of different forms and during the course of an audit you may be asked to sign several. Keep in mind the rule, "Never sign anything you don't understand." Here is a description of some of the more common forms:

- ▸ Form 2848—Power of Attorney. This must be filled out and signed by you if your organization wants to be represented in the matter by an attorney, CPA or similar person.

- ▸ Form 872 or 872A—Extension of the Statute of Limitations. The IRS has only a limited time in which to assess taxes (generally three years after the return is filed) and may request you to extend this period if an audit is in process. Unless the statute of limitations is on the verge of expiring, signing such a form is generally recommended since if you don't, the IRS can simply break off the audit and immediately make an enormous assessment. However, you should request Form 872 instead of 872A since 872 will extend the statute of limitations for only a specified period, while 872A will keep it open indefinitely. Doing so will prevent the IRS from letting the audit drag on forever. Generally they will substitute an 872 for an 872A upon request.

▸ Form 870—Consent to Immediate Assessment. Here's a form to watch out for—signing this means that your organization must pay the tax and cannot file a petition in the Tax Court. It's more or less a surrender. The organization could file a refund suit after paying the tax, but this is expensive.

(5) Principles of Handling an Audit

Every audit is different depending on the nature of the audit, the nature of the organization, and the personality of the examining agent. Nonetheless, there are a number of general guidelines which will help ensure the best possible outcome to the audit. These are general rules only and may have to be modified in special circumstances.

Also, this discussion is not intended to suggest that the treasurer should attempt to trick or thwart IRS agents. These agents are not the "enemy." On the contrary, following our recommendations will assist the IRS in speedily accomplishing what it originally planned to do when it began the audit while at the same time avoiding the creation of unnecessary problems for the organization.

▸ The first rule is "get professional assistance." Too many organizations try to save a few dollars by handling the audit themselves, only to wind up giving the IRS far more money than necessary. In such cases the organizations often cry "help" to their lawyer or CPA after the damage is done and pay a professional fee anyway—usually larger than what it would have been had advice been sought at the beginning. If the organization cannot afford a large fee, point this out to the tax adviser and have him merely "consult" while the organization does as much of the actual audit "leg work" as possible. Of course, professional help may not be necessary when the IRS request involves only a simple matter handled through the mails, such as an inquiry about whether a prior year's tax return was filed. But even when you get professional assistance, the remaining rules should be of interest since the organization will still have some involvement in the audit.

▸ The second rule is "never volunteer information." This rule is especially hard for nonprofit treasurers to follow since they tend to be friendly, helpful, and want to show that there is nothing to hide. Nonetheless, bite your tongue and limit responses to what was specifically requested. If the agent asks for your 2001 journal, give him that only. Don't toss in the checkbook, the ledger, the 2000 journal or anything else. If you verbally offer unsolicited information, something damaging may be inadvertently said. This happens more frequently than you think. If unsolicited documents are offered, the agent will naturally browse through them and may find something damaging, whereas if they weren't volunteered, there is a good chance he wouldn't have asked for them. In short, by volunteering information you make the audit bigger than necessary and thereby increase the organization's exposure to adverse results.

▸ Along the same line, beware of engaging in banter and casual conversation with the agent. It's okay to talk for a couple of minutes about weather or football, but be on alert if the conversation goes beyond this, either in terms of time or subject matter. The more time an agent spends on a job, the more tax dollars he is generally expected to produce. (This is officially denied by IRS, of course). Thus, wasting time in idle conversation puts pressure on the agent to assess a greater tax liability. But what's worse, agents are specifically trained to extract damaging information under the guise of innocent conversation. The idea is that you'll be talkative and have your guard down—and won't know you've said anything wrong until it's too late. Sounds bizarre, but it's true. For instance, the conversation might start out innocently enough on a discussion of the general economy, and continue like this (A=Agent, T=Treasurer):

A: "Times like this are tough on every kind of operation, even yours, I suppose."

T: "That's right, we've had our difficulties."

A: "Well, looking at your records, I see you've kept the level of contributions up pretty well. You must be a pretty good fundraiser and probably use some innovative strategies. I'm sure you just can't pass the hat anymore and get good results. Why, like this

$5,000.00 donation here, I doubt that it just dropped out of the blue. You have to work hard to get that kind of money. With this tight economy, I bet you even have to give some of those big contributors a little something extra. My brother works for a hospital and he says they had to lease all their equipment from this one guy who contributed $50,000.00. I suppose you have to do the same sort of thing."

T: "Yes, we have this airplane for disaster relief, but we fly our contributors around in it. The man who gave $15,000.00 uses it all the time."

BANG! TAX EXEMPTION REVOKED!

▸ While we have warned against giving the IRS unsolicited information, you should <u>generally</u> give them everything they specifically request. (There may be certain special exceptions such as confidential correspondence with an attorney.) Giving the information is a good idea because the organization can lose its exemption for withholding it, the IRS can usually get it anyway with a subpoena, and refusing to turn it over only makes the agent suspicious and results in an extended audit. However, if the agent removes original records from the premises, a receipt should be obtained as protection against loss by the IRS.

▸ Don't shout at, curse or otherwise treat the agent discourteously. They've been through it before and cannot be successfully intimidated. The only result may be the angry agent's assessment of an inflated tax deficiency.

▸ On the other hand, don't be overly friendly, just friendly. Shake the agent's hand, but don't buy him lunch, don't go drinking with him, don't give him a free book about your organization. The agent won't return the favor in the form of a smaller tax liability and may actually assess a bigger liability just to show that he hasn't been influenced by your kind treatment. Of course, where perquisites such as free coffee are available to all employees, the same should be made available to the agent or he may feel slighted. It's all a question of sensing the middle ground of courtesy without veering to the extremes of discourtesy or excessive friendliness.

▸ Upon arrival, the agent should, if possible, be given a separate office to work in so that he doesn't overhear employee conversations that might be damaging. A single person should be designated to handle all the agent's requests for records and information—to keep the agent from dealing with a variety of people, which creates confusion and increases the risk of volunteered information. If possible, the agent should not be allowed to browse freely through the file cabinets. Instead he should be asked to list specifically the items he wants to see. These items should be collected at the end of the day and put back so that the agent has to request specifically each item again the next day. The idea is that he won't request everything he had the day before and thus the audit will be limited as much as possible. Of course, these attempts to limit the audit should be made only with tact and courtesy.

▸ To sort or not to sort, that is the question. Is it better to give the agent invoices, checks and other records in a nice, neat order, or should they be given to him in a jumbled-up mess? There are proponents for each method—and the answer probably depends more on the agent's personality rather than on a hard and fast rule. Organized records make the audit shorter and may give the impression that your house is all in order—if they don't contain any damaging information. Disorganized records may cause the agent to give up in disgust—or may cause him to spend weeks at your office, confident that something amiss can be found in the mess. Unless you're a mind reader and can predict how the agent will react, the best bet is probably to give him the requested records "as is" rather than spending more of your own time sorting or unsorting them.

▸ The vast majority of agents are polite, but if you encounter a bully, contact the agent's supervisor. A few agents may also try some subtle blackmail on the layman treasurer. In such cases the agent asks for a concession on an issue and in exchange will offer to leave the organization alone on some other issue, which is groundless and farfetched anyway, but sounds scary to the layman. For instance, the agent might indicate that if you agree to his assessment of unrelated business income tax, he won't challenge the organization's exempt status. If such a challenge to exempt status would be groundless but the agent persists, either contact his supervisor or call the bluff by telling him to go ahead and write up his report. The agent will generally back off at this point, and if he doesn't, the matter can be quickly disposed of at the appeals level.

▸ During the course of an audit, you may be reviewing records and should be alert for allowable deductions or credits which weren't claimed on the tax return if a tax is involved. These should be pointed out to the agent and used to reduce the tax liability.

▸ Be cautious about making any kind of concession other than on a cut-and-dried matter which can't really be contested. A debatable issue generally should not be conceded except in exchange for an IRS concession or as part of the final settlement. In other words, don't be a nice guy and needlessly give away possible bargaining chips. Also, don't close your eyes to the effect of a concession on future years. Maybe a business activity produced only $500.00 of income in the year under audit, but is making thousands of dollars in subsequent years. Conceding that this is a taxable activity in the year under audit may also cause all future years to be taxable too. Likewise, consider the effect of any concession on the charitable contributions deduction of donors.

▸ Don't spend much time trying to get mercy by telling the agent about your organization's good works or dire need for funds. Agents never give discounts for a tear-jerking story.

▸ The IRS sometimes will begin an audit, drop out of sight for a few months, return—possibly in the form of a new individual, drop out of sight again and so forth. In many cases this is due to agent resignations or transfers and the resulting time lag before the audit can be reassigned. If you feel that the IRS has forgotten about your organization, don't call them. They will probably be back sooner or later, but there is always a chance your audit will slip between the cracks if you don't make the mistake of reminding them. If a new agent appears on the scene, he will probably duplicate some of the previous agent's work and may even start from scratch again. Be sure to speak up whenever you see a duplication of work by a successor agent. Sometimes the agent will then desist, but if he doesn't, there is not much you can do unless the duplication is enormous. In such a situation, contact the agent's supervisor.

K. CHANGE OF ASSOCIATION'S NAME

K.   Change of Association's Name

When an association officially changes its name, the treasurer should see that an announcement of the name change is sent to every government agency, tax authority, financial institution, insurance company and other body with which the association does business. After this, the treasurer should verify that those notified of the change actually use the new name in later correspondence.

Some banks and other agencies may require the filing of a sworn statement or a resolution adopted by the association's executive body, signed by the secretary and bearing the association's seal (if any). In addition, the treasurer should make sure an officer has notified the local Secretary of State. It may be necessary to amend the articles of incorporation so that the new name is officially registered, and for this the advice of an attorney may be needed.

Whatever is required, it is best to have the name change recorded properly and promptly in all necessary places. Failure to notify others of the name change may lead to an investment fund being tied up, a mix-up in tax records, or other unfortunate results.

L. CHANGING THE ASSOCIATION FINANCIAL SYSTEM

L.   Changing the Association Financial System

Occasionally the treasurer or other members may consider changing the association's accounting principles. Common examples of this are changing from one year-end to another (Chapter 4(H)), and changing from the cash basis to the accrual basis, or vice versa (Part II(F)). Other instances may include changing the carrying values of investments (cost or market value), changing the handling of bad debts (actual writeoff or estimated reserve), or changing the method of accounting for the flow of inventories held for resale (first in, first out; or last in, first out).

Such changes should not be made lightly. A treasurer who makes numerous changes in accounting principles can create many headaches for the association. A change in the year-end, for instance, means that there will be a "short period" (less than twelve months) income statement for the year of change— and since it is less than twelve months, comparing it to other years is difficult. In addition to this problem of evaluating the association's financial performance, there may also be disruptions in dues billing, budget making, and accounting for grant programs.

Multiple changes compound this confusion. Some people may begin to doubt the stability of the association or the accuracy of its financial statements.

However, this is not to say that changes should never be made. Erroneous methods, of course, should be corrected. Other changes may be desirable because they will simplify the treasurer's job. For example, an association on a June 30th year-end may find a December 31st year-end much easier because it coincides with W-2 Forms for employees and other report cut-off dates. Or an association as it becomes larger may want to adopt the accrual rather than the cash method of accounting (Part II(F)). If a change is made, these guidelines should be followed:

> ▸ Consult with others beforehand. This includes association officers or board members and the outside accountant or bookkeeper. These persons may have valuable input as to whether a change is desirable, and keeping them informed helps to avoid confusion after a change is made.

> ▸ If the association files a tax return (such as Form 990 or Form 990-T), it may be necessary to obtain Internal Revenue Service approval for certain changes. Filing Form 1128 may be necessary for changes in the year-end, and Form 3115 may have to be filed for other

changes in accounting practices. Professional assistance is usually needed here.

▸ The nature of the change should be fully explained on the financial statements. For changes of accounting methods, other than a change of the year-end, the difference in dollar amounts between the old method and the new one generally should be disclosed for the year of change.

▸ Financial statements for prior years should <u>not</u> be retroactively restated to show the accounting change (except when necessary to correct errors). Rather, the cumulative effect of the accounting change should be shown as an adjustment in the financial statement for the current year.

M. USING COMPUTERS

(1)   Pros and Cons of In-house Computers

(2)   When Adopting Computers is Appropriate

(3)   Making the Change

(4)   Using a Computer Service Bureau

M. Using Computers

Most small associations continue to keep their accounting records by hand, but with the prevalence of computers in our society, a few words on this subject are in order. Most of these comments do not apply to associations already "up and running" with a computer system, but apply instead to those which are now on a manual (i.e., hand-kept) system, but are considering a change to computers.

(1) Pros and Cons of In-house Computers

An in-house computer may save time in processing the accounting records once the start-up period has passed. (The start-up period, which could last several weeks, will require more time than before, not less.) Also, computers can perform other valuable functions in addition to accounting. For instance, they can be used for word processing (typing correspondence and newsletters) and for maintaining membership directories and mailing lists.

On the other hand, unless the association or treasurer already has a computer, there is the cost of purchasing the computer itself and also the software programs. There will be ongoing costs of supplies and repairs. (If a computer belonging to the treasurer is used, the association should consider what it will do about that when the treasurer's term is up.)

Apart from the monetary costs, time may be spent in learning to use the computer. Even if the treasurer is already well-trained, future treasurers may not be, and may not wish to devote the time required to learn. Also, if the treasurer is the only person familiar with the computer operation, these functions will grind to a halt when he is sick or on vacation.

(2) When Adopting Computers is Appropriate

If an association is having problems with its manual accounting system, the treasurer may be given advice to switch to a computer system, as if this will magically solve all problems. Such advice should be taken very cautiously.

Unless the association is bringing in someone who is well-trained both in accounting and computer operation, an in-house computer system usually should be adopted only if the manual accounting system is already functioning at least adequately (not necessarily excellently), except that it is too slow and time-consuming because of the volume of transactions.

Of course, where the manual system is working just fine, remember the proverb, "If it ain't broke, don't fix it!"

If the manual accounting system is in disarray, it is safe to assume that introducing a computer will only make the situation worse (with rare exceptions). The same mistakes will be made as under the manual system, except the computer will process those mistakes at lightning speed. Mistakes may also be harder to locate since they are hidden on a diskette or CD instead of being readily visible on paper.

Therefore, a computer generally should be introduced, if at all, only where orderliness and organization already exist.

(3) Making the Change

Because of the wide variety of computers and programs, it is impossible to begin to describe the particular manufacturers and models available and how they are operated. Furthermore, even if a current description were possible (it would fill several volumes), computer technology changes so rapidly that the description would be obsolete before this book reached the marketplace.

Therefore, unless the reader is already familiar with this area, advice should be obtained, not only from computer sales representatives, but also from treasurers of similar associations. A check of the telephone book *Yellow Pages* under "Associations" should give you some leads if you do not already know other treasurers.

During the first few weeks of computer use, the manual accounting system should also be maintained. This allows the accuracy of the computer operation to be checked and also provides a backup in case something goes wrong.

Your authors could tell you several "horror" stories where this important rule was not followed. In one situation every time a new transaction was entered on the computer, a previous transaction was erased. Since the manual system had been abandoned (although it had been working adequately before the computer was introduced), several weeks passed before the problem was discovered, and it was solved only after a painstaking reconstruction of records involving considerable time and expense.

In a second situation, not only was this rule broken (the one about continuing the manual system for the first few weeks), but also the rule about having an adequate manual system before changing to computers. Poor financial decisions resulting from the lack of accurate information eventually caused the organization to be liquidated. Even afterwards, no one knew for sure how much money had been lost, or why.

Sometimes it is advisable to keep backup copies of computer diskettes or CDs at another location, at least until the stored information is printed out or is no longer needed. Not only are computer diskettes and CDs subject to the same risks as paper records (*i.e.*, fire and flood), but because of the small size and fragility of diskettes and CDs, they are also subject to being accidentally erased, misplaced or damaged.

(4)   Using a Computer Service Bureau

A "service bureau" is a business which processes data for other organizations with its own computer. Using a service bureau can sometimes be a happy medium between a manual accounting system and an in-house computer. Computer knowledge on the part of the treasurer is not required, yet the service bureau may be able to compile a volume of transactions more rapidly than the treasurer could by hand, and will also produce financial statements.

However, the treasurer should weigh against these advantages the fees charged by the service bureau. Also, usually the treasurer will still have to spend time filling out input sheets, and may have to deliver them and pick up the finished product. Thus the time savings, if any, for a small association may not be significant.

When choosing a service bureau, examine the input sheets it uses and a sample of the financial statements it prepares to ensure that the format of each is appropriate for your association. The computer-generated financial statements may still have to be supplemented by explanatory footnotes (*see* Part II(I)(4)). Also, ask the service bureau about the safeguards it takes against input errors.

N. USING BANK PAYROLL SERVICES

N.   Using Bank Payroll Services

Perhaps one of the biggest favors that a treasurer can do for himself is to let a bank handle the association payroll. Most banks (or the service bureaus they use) will write the checks, calculate withholdings, maintain payroll records, deposit payroll taxes, and prepare payroll tax reports for a modest charge.

In some cases the treasurer may have difficulty reaching the association office to sign checks on each payday. The bank payroll service spares him those trips. And even where the treasurer or accountant is skilled in handling the payroll, the cost of using the bank service is generally far less than the hourly cost of having this done by someone in the organization. And where the treasurer is not experienced in handling the payroll, this service can be a godsend. Just having the bank prepare the payroll tax returns alone makes the service worthwhile because one of a small organization's biggest problems is in this area. Late or faultily-prepared returns or late deposits will result in severe penalties. The requirements are confusing and complex, so the inexperienced treasurer will frequently run into trouble (*see* Part II(C)).

Unless the treasurer and office staff can handle the payroll easily and accurately, an association should seriously consider letting the bank handle it.

O. UNRELATED BUSINESS INCOME TAX

(1)   Unrelated Activities

(2)   Exceptions

(3)   Exceptions to the Exceptions

(4)   Figuring the Tax

(5)   Tax Planning

O.   Unrelated Business Income Tax

(1)   Unrelated Activities

Although your organization may be known as "tax exempt," that exemption is not absolute even with respect to income taxes. Such taxes may still be owed on unrelated business income. Basically this is income, less allocable deductions, from an activity which is not substantially related to an organization's tax-exempt purposes, with certain exceptions.

Unless someone in the organization, such as the treasurer, is aware of the tax rules governing unrelated business income, the organization could conduct an activity without being aware of its tax liability—until receiving an IRS notice years later demanding immediate payment of accumulated taxes, interest and penalties.

Here is a list of some of the most common situations in which an organization could be taxed:

▸ The sale of member mailing lists to a commercial for-profit business.

▸ Fees received by an organization for sponsoring a member insurance program.

▸ Advertising space sold in the organization's magazine or journal.

▸ Income from travel tours sponsored by associations.

▸ Product endorsement fees.

▸ Business services such as data processing, product testing, debt collection, credit rating, or consulting sold to individual members of an association.

▸ Investment income of social clubs exempt under section 501(c)(7).

▸ Receipts from the general public for meals, *etc.*, of such social clubs.

▸ Pharmacy sales and lab tests for nonpatients of a hospital or clinic.

▸ Except in North Dakota, income from raffles and other games of chance (other than Bingo).

Of course, this list does not begin to cover all taxable activities. Nor is an activity always taxable merely because it appears on this list. An exception may apply, as discussed later in the chapter. Whenever there is doubt, consult your tax adviser.

For an activity not listed above, to determine whether it is taxable first requires an analysis of whether it is "substantially related" to the performance of the organization's tax-exempt function. The following are examples of income which is usually considered "related" and therefore nontaxable:

▸ Donations.

▸ Dues from members.

▸ The sale of an association magazine or journal containing articles related to the exempt purpose, such as a history magazine sold by an historical museum or association. (Advertising income, however, would be taxable.)

▸ Tuition charged for educational seminars by an association.

▸ Admission tickets sold for sporting events of a college or little league; and tickets to artistic performances of a college, ballet, opera, orchestra or similar organization.

▸ Sale of membership directories to members only.

▸ A hospital's or museum's operation of a parking lot, cafeteria or gift shop which is not advertised to the general public.

▸ The sale of books on the subject matter of the organization's exempt function. For instance, the sale by an art museum of books about art.

Obviously, the question of relatedness is often highly subjective and even your tax adviser may not know the answer for sure. Note that if the activity is unrelated, taxes are not avoided merely because the organization needs the funds or it spends the funds for a charitable purpose.

(2)   Exceptions

However, even activities that are unrelated may still be (but are not always) exempt from tax under one of the following exceptions for:

▸ Contributions or gifts to the organization. This exception often applies even if the donor's name or logo is featured at an event, but expert advice should be sought if this occurs.

▸ Irregular activities. These are activities which are one-shot or at least highly infrequent. Annual events are often considered irregular if the preparation, promotion and follow-up of the event cover only a short period.

▸ Activities in which substantially all the work is performed by volunteers.

- The sale of donated merchandise in a thrift store, benefit auction, rummage sale, charity book sale or similar activity.

- The mailing of low-cost promotional articles (costing $7.60 or less in 2002) such as pens or key chains as part of a contributions solicitation. Such items need to bear the organization's name or logo.

- Dividends, interest, royalties, annuities and capital gains.

- Real estate rents. Personal property rents are also exempt if part of the same rental package and are 10 percent or less of the total. However, if the personal property rents are over 50 percent of the rental package, then both the real and personal property portions are taxable. Real estate rents are also taxable if based on the net income from the rented property or if the organization performs services for the lessee other than traditional landlord services. Permissible services include providing utilities, collecting trash or cleaning public hallways. Tainted services might include maid, laundry or concession stand services. The IRS considers commercial parking lots, motels and warehouses as examples of activities where extra landlord services cause the rental income to be taxable.

- Conveniences for members, students, patients or employees of a section 501(c)(3) organization. An example is a university golf course for students and faculty only.

- Conventions and trade shows conducted by a section 501(c)(3), (4), (5) or (6) organization if related to the organization's purposes.

- Public entertainment activities, such as horse races, conducted by a section 501(c)(3), (4) or (5) organization in conjunction with a state or county fair.

- Bingo games, if legal under local law and not "ordinarily carried out on a commercial basis."

- The exchange or rental of member or donor mailing lists between nonprofit organizations to which deductible charitable contributions may be made.

- Funds set aside by veterans' organizations for member insurance or for a charitable purpose.

- Income from certain services provided by large hospitals to hospitals with facilities for 100 or fewer patients.

- Income from research performed for the government or performed by a college, hospital or organization formed to conduct fundamental research.

- Radio or TV stations operated by a religious order before May 27, 1959.

- Income from sales of uniforms or items out of vending machines or snack bars by a section 501(c)(4) employees' association organized before May 27, 1969.

(3)   Exceptions to the Exceptions

Even if your unrelated activity falls under one of the above exceptions, that does not automatically mean it's exempt from tax. Unfortunately, the law is complicated and there are four exceptions to the exceptions:

- *Controlled organizations provision.* Under this, interest, annuities, rents or royalties received from a 50 percent or more controlled subsidiary will be taxed to the parent in the same proportion that the subsidiary's unrelated taxable income bears to its total taxable income.

- *Membership organizations provision.* This applies to social clubs (section 501(c)(7)) and to employee beneficiary associations (501(c)(9)). Such organizations are taxed on all income except (a) income from members, (b) investment income set aside for a charitable purpose, and (c) gains on the sale of member-service property (such as a clubhouse) where the proceeds are reinvested in other member-service property within a three-year period.

- *Special pension rule.* A pension or profit-sharing plan is taxed on the income from any regular operating business and cannot use the volunteer exception.

- *Debt-financed tax.* This is by far the most complicated exception to the exception. If property is acquired by using a mortgage or other debt, income from the property (such as rents) may be taxable in the ratio that the current outstanding acquisition indebtedness bears to the current adjusted basis (original cost plus improvements, less depreciation). However, the tax does not apply to property used in an exempt function nor to certain property held for future use in an exempt function within ten years. Also, the tax does not apply where the debt consists of an inter-organizational loan, an FHA loan, or a mortgage on certain property acquired by gift or bequest.

Furthermore, the tax does not override the previously-mentioned exceptions for volunteer activities; the sale of donated merchandise; conveniences for members, students, patients or employees; and research activities. Finally, certain real estate activities of a pension plan or educational institution are also exempt.

(4)   Figuring the Tax

Once an activity is determined to be taxable, the amount of taxable income must be calculated. This generally consists of gross income from the activity less allocable deductions. However, in the case of advertising in a journal or newsletter, only direct advertising costs may be deducted; no allocation of editorial or general magazine costs may be made. If the rest of the magazine operates at a net loss, though, the loss may reduce advertising income (but not below zero). Each exempt organization is also allowed a special $1,000.00 deduction against its total unrelated business income.

The tax on the resulting amount is calculated using trust rates if your organization is a trust, or by using corporate rates if your organization is a corporation. Currently, through 2003, the corporate tax rate scale is as follows:

Taxable Income	Tax Rate On Increment
First $50,000	15%
Next $25,000	25%
Next $25,000	34%
Next $235,000	39%
Remainder	34%

The tax is reported on Form 990-T which is due on the 15th day of the fifth month after year-end. Prepayment of the tax at quarterly intervals throughout the year is generally required or else penalties may be imposed.

(5)   Tax Planning

We have already mentioned organizations that operate unaware of the unrelated business income tax until receiving a large assessment from the IRS years later. Obviously these organizations need to do tax planning.

Still other organizations are currently paying a tax, but are paying too much, again due to a lack of tax planning. In the vast majority of situations there is <u>some</u> way to reduce the tax. In many situations the tax can be eliminated altogether by careful planning. This is one area where the treasurer may be able to save substantial sums for the organization.

There is no excuse for not planning. Don't fall into the trap of thinking that the IRS will have mercy because your organization is a worthy cause or is short of funds. Experience has shown that the IRS grants no such mercy. Nor should you fall into the trap of relying on your accountant or lawyer to come up with tax planning ideas merely because they have been hired to do the organization's tax return or other work. Again, experience shows that many accountants and lawyers seldom bring unsolicited ideas to the attention of clients. For one thing, they're busy and therefore spend all their time on jobs they <u>have</u> to do, such as tax returns or client-initiated projects. Therefore, if you want tax planning, you usually have to ask for it specifically.

Some of the more common tax strategies are as follows:

▸ Use volunteers to conduct the activity.

▸ Make the activity substantially related to an exempt function by either restructuring the activity, amending the organization's exempt function as stated in its articles of incorporation, or creating a new subsidiary with a suitable exempt function to handle the activity.

▸ Structure the activity as a royalty arrangement by having it conducted by an unrelated third party with a percentage of the income paid back to the organization.

▸ Structure the activity as a real estate rental arrangement along the same lines as the above royalty arrangement. However, rents cannot be based on a project's <u>net</u> income, although they may be based on its <u>gross</u> income.

▸ Social clubs should set aside income for a charitable purpose, thereby avoiding tax on this amount. The funds can be withdrawn at a later date, but taxes will be imposed at that time.

▸ Exempt activities which operate at a loss may be turned into non-exempt activities for use in offsetting unrelated business income.

▸ The debt-financed tax may be avoided by setting aside certain property for use in an exempt function within ten years; by using an intermediary to incur the debt; by extending or renewing old debts instead of incurring new debt to acquire the property; and by obtaining funds from a stockbroker instead of borrowing funds. This is done by loaning marketable securities to the broker in exchange for cash collateral.

Don't attempt to implement a tax plan based on just this discussion, which was written to acquaint you with the <u>concepts</u> of planning and the <u>kinds</u> of problems that may be encountered. It doesn't go into all the complications and technicalities which must be handled in connection with the unrelated business income tax. Since the tax law may have changed since this book was written, you should consult the organization's tax adviser for complete details. Updated information may also be found on the Internet at: www.irs.gov.

P. FUND ACCOUNTING

P.　Fund Accounting

A nonprofit organization must choose whether to use single fund or multi-fund financial statements. A "fund" represents the organization's "net assets" or "net worth"—the difference between assets and liabilities. Under the single fund method there is only one fund balance account, and all other accounts—assets, liabilities, income and expense—are shown without any distinction as to whether transactions in the account are subject to spending restrictions imposed by donors. The single fund format is the simplest method of keeping the books and is similar to for-profit accounting.

However, many nonprofit entities have traditionally followed the more complex practice of multi-fund accounting. Here there are several fund balances, and each fund has a separate set of books containing its own separate asset, liability, income and expense accounts. The reason for separate funds is that some assets are subject to donor restrictions on how they may be spent, while other assets may be used in any manner that the organization sees fit.

Let us illustrate the difference between single and multi-fund accounting with an example. Suppose an organization has $1,000.00 of cash (of which $300.00 has been earmarked by donors for a special project), $500.00 of furniture, $600.00 of stocks and bonds, and a liability to the bank of $200.00. The stocks and bonds were donated, subject to the restriction that only the interest and dividends thereon could be spent for operations. The stocks and bonds themselves must be held forever instead of spent (this is called an "endowment").

Under the single fund method, the balance sheet (or Statement of Financial Position) would appear as follows:

<u>ASSETS</u>

Cash	$1,000
Stocks and Bonds	600
Furniture	500
Total	$2,100

<u>LIABILITIES AND FUND BALANCE</u>

Bank Loan	$ 200
Restricted Fund Balance	300
Unrestricted Fund Balance	1,600
Total	$2,100

Note, however, that this manner of presentation does not adequately inform financial statement readers about the donor-imposed restrictions on the stocks and bonds and $300.00 of the cash. Therefore, many nonprofit entities have segregated such assets into separate funds. Thus there would be three balance sheets instead of one:

	UNRESTRICTED	RESTRICTED	ENDOWMENT
ASSETS:			
Cash	$ 700	$ 300	
Stocks and Bonds			$ 600
Furniture	500		
Total	$ 1,200	$ 300	$ 600
LIABILITIES & FUND BALANCE:			
Bank Loan	$ 200		
Restricted Fund Balance		$ 300	
Fund Balance	1,000		$ 600
Total	$ 1,200	$ 300	$ 600

Note that the total of the three separate columns ($1,200.00+$300.00+$600.00) equals the $2,100.00 total under the single fund method of accounting.

Financial statement readers are now able to see that the stocks and bonds and $300.00 of the cash cannot be used to finance general operations. This information can be essential if the organization's financial condition is being evaluated for purposes of making budgets, extending grants or approving loans.

The price of this additional information, though, is added complexity. This complexity can increase considerably where more funds exist. Wouldn't it be easier to just use the single fund method and include footnotes explaining the donor restrictions on the stocks and bonds and $300.00 of cash? The answer, of course, is yes. If the treasurer has complete flexibility in designing the accounting system, the single fund method—with explanatory footnotes—may be used if desired. In many situations, though, conditions attached to a grant or loan may require the use of multi-fund accounting. Or the organization may have been on the multi-fund system for so long that a change would be too difficult to make or explain.

If the organization has decided to use the multi-fund method, the nature of the various funds must be determined. Some of the more common funds are:

- Unrestricted fund—These are assets, other than major fixed assets, that are not subject to donor restrictions. Such assets may be spent for any purpose.

- Restricted fund—These are assets, other than major fixed assets, which are subject to donor restrictions. These assets can be spent only for purposes specified by the donor. For instance, the donor to an association may specify that the money is to be used only for an emergency fund to assist members in distress.

- Plant fund—These are major fixed assets such as buildings.

- Endowment fund—This is a special type of restricted fund where the assets must be invested for an extended period (usually forever), and only the investment income thereon may be spent. Sometimes the income may be spent for any purpose and sometimes the income is restricted to a specific purpose.

Once the number and nature of the various funds has been determined, a separate set of records must be established for each fund. Some organizations combine the various fund accounts into a single ledger book, but this is a poor practice and leads to confusion. Completely separate ledgers and journals should be kept for each fund.

Transactions are recorded as if each fund was a separate organization all by itself. Each fund has its own assets, liabilities, fund balance, income, expenses and net profit or loss.

There are certain unique transactions caused by the nature of multi-fund accounting. For instance, an endowment arrangement may be terminated by the donor, enabling the asset to be transferred to the unrestricted fund. Transfers should never be shown as items of income or expense since they do not originate outside the organization. Instead they should be recorded as increases or decreases in the applicable fund balances. On the income statement for each fund, transfers are shown below the net income line but above the ending fund balance line.

In addition, income earned on endowment fund assets requires special treatment. If the income may be spent only for a specified purpose, the income is recorded in the restricted fund (not in the endowment fund). If the income may be spent for any purpose, then it is recorded as income directly in the unrestricted fund.

Continuing with the example shown at the beginning of the chapter, suppose the organization receives $500.00 of donations, of which $200.00 is restricted for a special project and in fact is spent for that purpose during the year. Dues income is $300.00 and office expenses are $200.00. Interest expense is $20.00. In addition, the stocks and bonds in the endowment fund earn $100.00, which may be spent for any purpose. Finally, because of changed circumstances the endowment donor has authorized the transfer of $150.00 from the principal of the endowment fund to the unrestricted fund to finance general operations.

Income statements (or Statement of Activities) for the funds are as follows:

	UNRESTRICTED	RESTRICTED	ENDOWMENT
Donations	$ 300	$ 200	
Dues	300		
Investment income	100		
Office expenses	(200)		
Interest expense	(20)		
Restricted project expense		(200)	
Net income	$ 480	-0-	-0-
Beginning Fund Balance	1,000	-0-	600
Transfer to Unrestricted Fund	150		(150)
Ending Fund Balance	$ 1,630	-0-	$ 450

Note that no income is recorded in the endowment fund even though the stocks and bonds in the account earned $100.00. Since the income may be spent for any purpose, it is shown in the unrestricted fund. If, however, the $100.00 earned on the stocks and bonds were restricted on how it could be spent, then the income would be recorded in the restricted fund instead.

If stocks in the endowment fund are sold, a question arises as to how capital gains and losses are treated. Are they treated as adjustments to the fund balance (which means that they stay in the endowment fund), or as an item of income or expense (which means that they go into the unrestricted or restricted funds as would a dividend)? The answer will vary. Under the laws of many states, a gain or loss would be treated as an increase or decrease in the endowment fund balance, assuming that the endowment agreement does not provide otherwise. Usually, though, the agreement either specifically states how gains and losses will be accounted for, or states that the organization's governing board can select the accounting treatment of its choice. Where a choice is available, the modern preference is to treat capital gains and losses as items of income and expense rather than as adjustments to the fund balance.

Cash set aside by the organization's governing board for a special purpose is not included with "restricted funds" since the board can change its mind at any time and lift the reservation. Only where the limitations on use are imposed by donors or grantors is money included in "restricted funds." However, a footnote should be used to inform financial statement readers of any amounts set aside by the board for a special purpose.

Q. PRIVATE FOUNDATIONS

(1)   Definition

(2)   Penalty Taxes

(3)   Reporting Requirements

Q. Private Foundations

If your organization is exempt under section 501(c)(3), you must be aware of the private foundation rules. "Private foundation" is the term used for certain types of section 501(c)(3) organizations which indicates that they are subject to additional regulations and penalties because they are not "public." A donor's contribution tax deduction may also be restricted (*see* Part II(R)(2) and (3)). Private foundation status isn't always a big problem, but organizations should avoid being classified as such if possible. When private foundation status is unavoidable, the treasurer should carefully monitor compliance with the foundation rules—because failure to comply can sometimes be catastrophic.

> WARNING: The subject of private foundations is highly complex—much more so than the simplified discussion presented here. Whenever in doubt, consult your tax adviser. Updated information can also be found on the Internet at: http://www.irs.gov.

(1) Definition

Organizations exempt under sections other than 501(c)(3) are not private foundations and do not have to worry about these rules.

A private foundation is defined as an organization exempt under section 501(c)(3), other than:

- ▸ A church.
- ▸ A school, college or university, or qualifying support organization.
- ▸ A hospital or qualifying medical research organization.
- ▸ A governmental unit.
- ▸ A U.S. organization that has received at least one-third of its support over the four preceding years (taken together) from government grants or contributions from the general public. The contributions of any one nongovernmental donor are not counted in the numerator of the one-third requirement to the extent they exceed two percent (2%) of total support, but are included in the denominator.

However, "unusual and unexpected" grants and contributions can be excluded from both numerator and denominator.

▸ An organization that: (a) receives more than one-third of its support from grants, contributions or membership fees, or from income from the sale of goods and services which is not an unrelated trade or business (*see* Part II(O)), and (b) receives one-third or less of its support from investment income and unrelated business taxable income. Both tests are computed by using the totals for the four preceding years taken together. Furthermore, receipts from "disqualified persons" are not counted in the numerator of the first test. ("Disqualified persons" are defined as foundation managers, or contributors of over $5,000.00 if this exceeds two percent (2%) of total contributions, or a party related to such a person.) When computing income from the sale of goods and services which is not unrelated business income, receipts from any single person or entity are disregarded to the extent they exceed the greater of $5,000.00 or one percent (1%) of the organization's support.

▸ An organization operated exclusively to support one of the above organizations.

▸ An organization operated exclusively for testing for public safety.

Even if your section 501(c)(3) organization manages to fall under one of the above exceptions, it will still be considered a private foundation unless it notifies the IRS to the contrary within 15 months after the organization is formed (for further information see IRS Form 1023). However, churches don't have to make this notification.

(2)   Penalty Taxes

If your organization is unfortunate enough to be classified as a private foundation, it may become subject to a tax on net investment income (either 1% or 2%), and also to substantial penalties (up to 200%) on the five following items:

▸ Transactions with "disqualified persons" (defined above).

▸ Failure to annually distribute a minimum amount of income, generally five percent (5%) of the foundation's net investment assets.

▸ Excess investments in a business. Generally, a foundation plus its disqualified persons cannot own over twenty percent (20%) of a corporation's stock, but this can be increased to thirty-five percent

(35%) with IRS permission. At any rate the foundation by itself may own two percent (2%) or less.

▸ Risky investments such as commodity futures, stock options or oil wells.

▸ Prohibited expenditures such as lobbying; political campaign activities; travel or study grants to an individual unless IRS requirements are met; or payments for a noncharitable purpose.

Furthermore, if the foundation terminates by reason of liquidation, conversion to a public charity, or flagrant acts subject to one of the above penalties, a termination tax may be imposed equal to the lesser of the foundation's net assets or the total tax benefit resulting from its exempt status since inception. However, the IRS may waive this tax if it is satisfied that the foundation's assets will continue to be used for charitable purposes.

(3)   Reporting Requirements

Private foundations file Form 990-PF as their annual tax return, which is due by the 15th day of the fifth month after year-end (May 15th for a calendar-year organization). The penalty for late filing is $20.00 a day. For obtaining proof of filing with the IRS for Form 990-PF, or for obtaining extensions of time to file using Form 8868, follow the same instructions as for Form 990 which is covered at Part II(B)(1)(d). Private foundations, like other tax-exempt organizations, must also make their tax documents available for public inspection. For further information see Part I, Chapter 6(H).

R. CHARITABLE CONTRIBUTIONS

(1)   Eligible Organizations

(2)   Amount of the Deduction
      (a)   Individual Donors
      (b)   Corporate Donors

(3)   Percentage Limitations
      (a)   Individual Donors
      (b)   Corporate Donors

(4)   Tax Planning

(5)   Deferred Contributions

(6)   Other Matters

R.   CHARITABLE CONTRIBUTIONS

Treasurers are sometimes asked about the tax rules governing charitable contributions to the organization. This chapter is designed to help you answer those questions—and to help you maximize the contributions to your organization by showing prospective donors how painless contributions can sometimes be after taking tax benefits into account. As with any other tax subject, the rules are often confusing and are also changed by Congress every few years. Thus, this chapter can only provide a general overview together with ideas for tax planning. If the amount of the contribution is large, either the organization or the donor should obtain professional assistance. Updated information can also be found on the Internet at: www.irs.gov.

The rules governing contributions are best looked at in a three-step sequence. First, is the organization eligible to receive deductible contributions? Second, what is the amount of the deduction? Third, are there any percentage limits on the donor's total contributions? These three issues are discussed in the following sections.

(1)   Eligible Organizations

The first question is whether donors can get a tax deduction for contributions to your organization. In order for them to do so, your organization must be tax exempt. But that is not enough—contrary to popular belief, not every type of nonprofit or tax-exempt organization qualifies for the deductibility feature.

Here are the types of organizations to which deductible contributions can be made:

- A national, state or local government body in the United States.
- A section 501(c)(3) organization based in the United States. (This is one formed for religious, charitable, scientific, literary or educational purposes, to promote amateur sports or to prevent cruelty to children or animals.)
- An organization of war veterans or an auxiliary unit or foundation thereof. (Section 501(c)(19).)
- A fraternity or sorority organized in the United States, but only if the donation is used for religious, charitable, scientific, literary or educational purposes, or for the prevention of cruelty to children or animals. Thus, general contributions or building fund contributions do

not qualify for a deduction. However, funds used for a library room or for student scholarships probably would qualify.

IMPORTANT NOTE: Only <u>individual</u> donors can make such deductible contributions. Corporations, trusts and partnerships can never receive a deduction for contributions to fraternities or sororities.

▸ A nonprofit cemetery or burial association.

For tax-exempt organizations averaging more than $100,000.00 of annual gross receipts and which do not fall into one of the above categories (in other words, donations to the organization are <u>not</u> tax deductible as charitable contributions), all fundraising and membership solicitations must contain a statement advising persons that their payments are not deductible as charitable contributions. Since there are substantial penalties for failing to give this statement, many such organizations include it with any correspondence asking for money, including invoices for sales and dues. To avoid reprinting these forms, a small sticker containing the statement can simply be attached. Of course, even if payments are not tax deductible as charitable contributions, under appropriate circumstances certain payments may be deducted as business expenses, such as dues paid to a trade association by a business member.

(2) Amount of the Deduction

If your organization possesses the deductibility feature, the next step is to determine the <u>dollar</u> <u>amount</u> of the donor's deduction. This depends on the nature of the contributor, the nature of the organization and the nature of the property given.

(a) *Individual Donors*: The deduction for cash gifts, of course, is simply the amount given. For property gifts, the deduction generally is the lower of market value or adjusted cost (original cost less tax depreciation taken, if any). However, a higher deduction can be obtained for property in certain instances. This occurs where the property is appreciated in value and would produce a long-term capital gain if sold. (Property is of the long-term capital variety if it is owned more than one year and is not an item of inventory held for sale in the regular course of business.) For such property, the deduction is the fully appreciated value less the following amounts:

▸ Ordinary income element. This is any part of the gain that would be ordinary (as opposed to capital) if the property was sold. The most common example is depreciation recapture—generally any tax depreciation taken on personal (movable) property and part of the accelerated depreciation (if any) taken on real estate. Depreciation recapture, however, will never exceed the appreciation in the property. Common examples of this are contributions to charity of cars previously used for business, or of computers or office equipment previously deducted as business expenses. In these situations donors usually do not get to deduct the full value.

▸ The long-term capital gain element is subtracted where the property is donated to certain private foundations (Part II(Q)), or where the property is tangible personal property and is not used by the organization in an exempt function. Tangible personal property is property other than real estate or intangible property (such as stocks and bonds). Donated medical equipment or office furniture could be used by a clinic in its exempt function, but a sailboat or airplane probably could not be (unless it was used as an air ambulance, for instance). Other examples could be a piano used by a church, or artwork put on long-term public display. If your organization turns around and sells the property, though, it is not used in an exempt function, regardless of how the proceeds are used.

EXAMPLE: John Doe gives a stamp collection to his church. It cost $1,000.00 several years ago and is worth $6,000.00. Since the stamps are tangible personal property and the church presumably can't use them in an exempt function, the deduction is only $1,000.00. Had the donated property instead been real estate or shares of stock held more than one year, the deduction would be the full $6,000.00. Or if John Doe had given the stamp collection to a section 501(c)(3) philatelic society, or to a museum or library where the stamps would be displayed, then possibly the full $6,000.00 could be deducted.

COMMON SITUATION: Certain types of organizations such as thrift stores or churches frequently receive used household items such as clothes, books and appliances. Most organizations give the donor a receipt showing the type of property donated but do not show a valuation—because the donor has the responsibility of setting the value. If a donor does ask you to write down a value, your first response should be that the donor is supposed to use his best estimate. But if the donor insists that you do it, go ahead and help him make an estimate but point out that it won't bind the IRS. As a general rule, the IRS is very tight and won't allow the deduction for used clothes or furnishings to exceed ten to twenty percent (10%–20%) of the original cost—unless the donor has an independent appraisal or can otherwise prove a higher value. Donors must file Form 8283 with their tax returns if aggregate total property donations for the year, for all organizations combined, is $500 or more.

(b) *Corporate Donors:* Corporate donors receive the same amount for deductions as individuals, except that a corporation (other than an "S" corporation which files Form 1120S as its tax return) can obtain a deduction for the cost plus one-half of the appreciation, but not to exceed twice the cost of the following types of property:

▸ Inventory donated to and used by an organization caring for the sick, needy or infants, such as a clinic, charity or day-care center, or under certain circumstances, computer equipment donated to a school or public library.

▸ New research and development equipment which is manufactured by the donor and contributed to a college, university or nonprofit research organization for use in scientific research.

(3)   Percentage Limitations

After establishing the dollar amount of the deduction for a single gift, the next problem is determining whether a percentage limit applies to the donor's total contributions. Again, this depends on the nature of the contributor, the nature of the organization and the nature of the property given.

(a) *Individual Donors:* The total deduction for an individual donor's contributions to all organizations is limited to fifty percent (50%) of adjusted gross income. Excess contributions can be carried forward and deducted in one of the next five years to the extent that contributions in that year are less than the fifty percent (50%) limit.

However, the total deduction for an individual's contributions to certain private foundations (Part II(Q)) is limited to thirty percent (30%) of adjusted gross income for cash or ordinary income property, and twenty percent (20%) for capital gains property.

Finally, an individual's total deduction for contributions of appreciated long-term capital gains property is limited to the lesser of thirty percent (30%) of adjusted gross income or whatever is left of the fifty percent (50%) limit after taking into account non-capital-gain contributions. However, any excess may be carried forward five years. There is also a special provision which allows the thirty percent (30%) limit to be waived if the donor elects to deduct only his adjusted cost in the property instead of the full fair market value.

(b) *Corporate Donors:* The percentage limitations are completely different for corporations (other than "S" corporations). Instead of three limits—fifty percent (50%), twenty percent (20%) and thirty percent (30%)—there is only one: Ten percent (10%) of taxable income before the dividends-received deduction, net operating loss carrybacks, and certain other special deductions. Excess amounts may be carried forward and utilized in one of the five following years to the extent that current contributions in that year are less than ten percent (10%). In the case of an "S" corporation, there is no percentage limit at the corporate level. Each stockholder personally deducts his share of the contribution, subject to the percentage limitations for individuals.

(4)   Tax Planning

There is no better way to satisfy donors—and to get larger donations—than by cutting the cost of contributions with special tax-saving ideas. Here are a few for the treasurer to keep in mind:

‣ If your organization is not a private foundation, suggest that the donor contribute appreciated long-term capital gains property, other than tangible personal property which won't be used in an exempt function. Stocks and real estate are ideal candidates. The advantage is that the full appreciated value is deductible but no tax has to be paid on the appreciated gain. If the donor sold the property and contributed cash instead, the gain would be taxed to the donor.

‣ For the same reason, any investment property which has declined in value below cost should never be contributed. Instead it should be sold by the donor and cash contributed instead since a sale allows the donor to obtain the benefits of the tax loss. No tax loss is allowed on a contribution of property.

‣ If problems are caused by the thirty percent (30%) limit on donations of appreciated long-term capital gains property by individuals, suggest making the election to use the fifty percent (50%) limit instead—which requires that the deduction be limited to the adjusted cost. This may be useful where the carryover of the excess over thirty percent (30%) can't be fully deducted within the next five years; where the donor is in a high tax bracket now but won't be in future years (after retirement, for instance); or where the appreciation is small in relation to the total value of the property.

‣ If a corporate donor has problems because of the ten percent (10%) limit, consider having the donor contribute inventory acquired during the current year—which is deductible as a cost of goods sold and is not subject to the percentage limit for other contributions.

▸ Another method of avoiding the percentage limits in the case of a corporation consists of having the corporation give one of its employees a bonus equal to the desired contribution; the employee then turns around and contributes the money. The bonus is generally deductible in full by the corporation while the employee usually has a fifty percent (50%) contribution limit—compared to a ten percent (10%) limit if the corporation made the contribution directly. Note that the IRS could question this technique, especially if the bonus is large or is used to pay a corporate pledge.

▸ Make contributions in the right year. If the donor—whether individual or corporate—fluctuates between high and low tax brackets over the years, the biggest tax savings will come from making contributions in the high bracket years. Likewise, if an excess contributions carryover is expiring in the current year, contributions planned for the current year should be deferred until next year if possible to allow maximum utilization of the carryover in the current year.

▸ Corporate donors using the accrual method (Part II(F)) have the privilege of deducting contributions in the current year even though payment is delayed until two and one-half months after the end of the year. Board of directors approval is required prior to year-end. If potential corporate donors claim they don't have the cash right now, point this out!

▸ If the donor needs lifetime benefits from the property, suggest a deferred contribution as discussed below.

(5)   Deferred Contributions

Until now our discussion has centered on outright gifts of cash or other property where your organization receives immediate ownership. However, in many cases where the property is substantial—a home, a farm or a large investment portfolio, for instance—the donor is unwilling to give it unless certain lifetime benefits can be retained. The solution to this problem is a deferred gift. If properly done, the donor gets an immediate deduction for the discounted value of the gift, using IRS actuarial tables. In addition, the donor (and spouse) can use the property for life—in the case of a home or farm—or can get a lifetime income from one of the following vehicles:

▸ Annuity trust. Here the donor receives a <u>fixed amount</u> each year which never varies. If the trust invests in municipal bonds, the donor's lifetime income can be tax-free.

- Unitrust. Here the donor receives a <u>fixed percentage</u> of the contributed property's value, as determined annually. If the property's value goes up, so does the donor's income. If the value goes down, so does the income.

- Pooled income fund. Here the donor receives a fluctuating annual income based on the earnings of a fund which owns property received from a number of donors.

Deferred gifts to charity have many tax-saving attractions, but are also quite complicated and usually require assistance from a professional tax adviser.

(6) Other Matters

To complete our discussion of charitable contributions, here are a few other points worth noting:

- Individuals can obtain a deduction for estate tax purposes—but not for income tax purposes—if a bequest is left to charity in the donor's will.

- There is no deduction for allowing your organization to use property rent-free. Nor do volunteers get any deduction for the value of their donated time.

- Out-of-pocket expenses incurred in charitable volunteer work are usually deductible if there is no significant element of personal recreation for the donor. This includes meals, transportation, lodging, phone calls and supplies. Such expenses must be adequately documented by receipts, canceled checks and an expense diary. In the case of automobile usage, a standard mileage rate prescribed by law may be deducted (in 2003 it was 14 cents per mile), or the actual cost of gas and oil may be used, if higher. Note that this charitable mileage rate is considerably different from the IRS mileage rate for business use.

- For contributions other than money or publicly-traded stock, for which a deduction in excess of $5,000.00 will be claimed (or $10,000.00 in the case of nonpublicly-traded stock), the donor must obtain an independent appraisal and file Schedule B of Form 8283 with his tax return. A copy of Form 8283 is also given to the organization.

- For any of the contributions in the preceding paragraph, if the organization disposes of the property within two years after the donation, it must file Form 8282 with the IRS within 90 days and provide a copy to the donor.

▸ No deduction is allowed for purchasing raffle or lottery tickets. Nor is the cost of dinner tickets or admission fees deductible as contributions unless it can be proven that the amount paid exceeds the value of the dinner or event—and then only the excess is deductible. This rule applies even if the person does not attend the dinner or event unless the person returns the ticket to your organization in time to resell it. However, certain business purchasers may be able to deduct dinner or admission tickets as a business expense.

▸ *See* Chapter 6(G) for information on the statements which you must provide to donors where something is received in return for the contribution or where any contribution is $250.00 or larger.

THE AUTHORS

Joseph M. Galloway received his law and M.B.A. degrees from Drake University in 1978, and was a tax manager with the accounting firm of Deloitte Haskins & Sells until 1983, when he established his own law practice in Des Moines, Iowa. A Certified Public Accountant, an attorney in the Iowa and Nebraska bar associations, and a Chartered Life Underwriter, Mr. Galloway is the author of numerous articles on tax questions; the book, *The Unrelated Business Income Tax* (John Wiley & Sons, 1982); and co-author (with Clair J. Galloway) of *Handbook of Accounting for Insurance Companies* (McGraw-Hill, 1986).

Alden Todd, a journalist and freelance writer since 1946, was an editor and publications director with the accounting firm of Deloitte Haskins & Sells from 1968 to 1983, when he returned to freelance writing. He is the author of six nonfiction books: *Finding Facts Fast* (Morrow 1972, Ten Speed Press 1979); *Favorite Subjects in Western Art* (Dutton 1968); *Richard Montgomery, Rebel of 1775* (McKay 1967); *A Spark Lighted in Portland* (McGraw-Hill 1966); *Justice on Trial: The Case of Louis D. Brandeis* (McGraw-Hill 1964); *Abandoned: The Story of the Greely Arctic Expedition* (McGraw-Hill 1961).

Both authors have served several times as treasurers of associations, and have seen how many mistakes are made by well-meaning amateurs who become treasurers of organizations. They know how badly a practical guide of this type is needed. Mr. Galloway brings to this project the knowledge and experience of the practitioner trained in accounting, law and the world of business. Mr. Todd, four times treasurer of the American Society of Journalists and Authors, has learned at close hand how many otherwise capable people are like babes in the woods when a treasurership is thrust upon them.

INDEX

Accounting year, 26, 42-43
Accrual method accounting, 139
Accuracy in reporting, 17, 23
Advances on salary, 93, 99
Annual duties, 107, 112
Annual financial report preparation, 153
Annual reporting, 81, 114, 117
Articles of incorporation, 70, 107-111, 121, 171, 187
Assessments, special, 85, 89
Assistant treasurer, 8, 16
Audit, annual, 44, 59, 159
Authorized signatures, 17, 19-20

Bad-debt writeoff, 54
Balance sheet, 142, 152-155, 159, 190
Bank balance, interpretation of, 17, 24
Bank deposit records, 30
Bank statement, reconciling, 38
Banks, investment funds, 71, 74
Benefits, non-salary, 7, 93, 97
Bills, keeping originals, 71, 74
Bills paid, 31, 68
Budget analysis, 44, 51-52, 56-57, 145
Budgeting, 45-49
Bylaws, 5, 20, 27, 70, 91, 107-108, 111, 160

CPA services: audit, compilation, review, 60, 159
Cash disbursements, controls over, 44, 55
Cash donations, 44, 55
Cash or accrual method accounting, 139
Cash receipts, controls over, 44, 52
Cash receipts, 18, 26, 30-31, 33-36, 44, 52-53, 70, 139
Changing the financial system, 172-173
Charitable contributions, 92, 105, 115, 120-121, 169, 184, 199-201, 206

Checkbook protection, 144, 147
Checkbook records, 26-27
Checkbook records, deposits, 26
Checklist of reports and payments, 105, 131-134
Churches and religious organizations, 125-126
Computer service bureau, 175, 178
Computers, appropriate adoption point, 175-177
Computers, changing to, 177
Computers, in-house-pros and cons, 175-177
Contributions, charitable, 81, 92, 115, 120-121, 169, 184, 199-201, 206
Custody of books and records, 44, 67

Delinquents, 7, 85, 90
Discrimination, 101, 114, 120, 124
Double entry bookkeeping, 135-137, 150
Dues, amount of, 89
Dues collection, 68, 85, 89-90
Dues, flat or variable, 85-86
Dues, payment frequency, 87
Dues refunds, 85, 88
Dues, setting and changing, 85
Dues year, 85, 88
Duplicate summary records, 26, 36

Earnings and deductions records, 78, 93, 95
Employer identification number, 94, 114-115
Errors, ways of finding, 39-40, 150
Expected income, 44-45, 65
Expenditures records, 27-30
Expense allowance, 104

Facsimile signatures, 17, 20
Fellowship expenses, 44, 63-64
Fidelity bonds, 44, 60
Files, action guides to, 44, 69
Files cleaning, 44, 69
Filing system, 44, 67
Financial educator, treasurer's role, 17, 22
Financial reports, board attention to, 17, 21
Financial reports, clarity of, 17, 21

Financial reports, failure to deliver, 12, 13
Finding errors, 26, 40, 60, 105, 149-151
Fiscal year, 23, 35, 42, 64, 78, 97
Footnote disclosures, 152, 158, 160
Forms W-2 at year-end, 93, 99
Foundations, private, 195-198, 202
Free admissions, giveaways, 44, 63
Fund accounting, 105, 189-190

Hiring new employees, 93, 101

IRS audit, 105, 161-162
IRS audit, cutting red tape, 163
IRS audit, forms to sign, 164
IRS audit, immunity from, 163
IRS audit, principles of handling, 165
In-and-out accounts, 26, 35
Income statement, 152-158, 173, 192
Income tax withholding, 125-127
Incorporation or not, 108
Insurance company or agency, 60, 80
Internal controls, 5, 44, 49-51
Investing idle cash, 44, 65

Kiting, 54-55

Landlord, 6, 71, 73, 75-76, 80, 184
Liaison between old and new treasurers, 18
Lapping, 53-54
"Lost check" swindle, 144, 146

Management of the organization, 109
Monitoring financial trends, 44, 62

Name-change notifications, 171
Name of organization, 109
New accounts, starting, 26, 35
New organization, forming, 107-108
Non-wage payments, 93, 103

Office economies, 93, 100
Office work load, controlling the, 44, 64

Paying payroll taxes, 125, 128
Payroll frauds, 144-145
Payroll taxes, 18, 47, 68, 79, 94, 105, 115, 119-120, 125-128, 162, 180
Payroll taxes, paying, 125, 128
Payroll taxes, reporting, 68
Permits and exemptions, 107, 112
Personnel file, employee, 92, 99
Petty cash, controls over, 44, 58
Place of organization, 107-108
"Plugging" unbalanced reconciliation, 26, 40
Political activities, 114, 120, 122-123
Prenumbered documents, 44, 59
Private foundations, 105, 110, 118, 123, 195-196, 198, 202
Private persons, benefits to, 114, 120, 122
Prompt check deposit, 29, 61
Public inspection of tax documents, 71, 83

References for former employees, 93, 102
Reimbursement of expenses, 44, 62
Repeated expenses, monitoring, 62
Reports to membership, 85, 91
Retention of documents, 44, 69

Safeguarding cash in public place, 44, 61
Salaries and benefits, 44, 64
Salaries of employees, 44, 64
Secretary of state, 71, 76, 81, 109, 111-112, 132, 171
Separation of duties, 44, 52-53
Single entry bookkeeping, 135-136
Single or double entry bookkeeping, 105, 135-136
Social Security (FICA) taxes, 6, 77, 94, 126-130
Soliciting funds, 71, 81

Tax agencies, federal and state, 6, 71, 77
Tax deductibility of dues, 92
Tax-exempt status, 70, 78, 105, 108, 114-116, 120, 132, 162
Tax-exempt status, retaining of, 114, 120

Tenant, 6, 65, 75-76, 80
Theft prevention, 145
Timely payment, 6, 93, 99
Treasurer, compensation, 24
Treasurer, duties of, xi
Treasurer, reimbursement, 24
Treasurer, selection of, 8-9, 12, 16

Unemployment claims, 93, 103
Unemployment tax, 70, 103, 126, 128-130
Unrelated activities, 114, 120-121, 181-182
Unrelated business income tax, 105, 168, 181-182, 186, 188, 209

Vendors, reviewing and paying bills, 71-72

"Watch List", 85, 91

9 780595 272624